Additional Praise for *The New Nature of Business*

"This must-read book for any business leader offers an inspiring blueprint for harmonizing business success with sustainable, inclusive prosperity."

—**Francisco Veloso,** *dean, INSEAD*

"We are blind to how much financial capital entirely depends on natural and social capitals. This book is an inspiring story of corporate lives evidencing that it is concretely both possible and urgent to change our economics."

—**Emmanuel Faber,** *chairman, International Sustainability Standards Board*

"What is the purpose of a company? Whom should it serve? Shareholders, employees, customers, community, or the planet? André takes us on an exciting journey through his and his family's stewardship of Roche. Through the ups and downs they experienced, he reaches the answer: a company is nothing if it doesn't provide returns for everyone and everything it affects."

—**Mo Ibrahim,** *founder, Mo Ibrahim Foundation*

ANDRÉ HOFFMANN | PETER VANHAM

THE
NEW NATURE
OF BUSINESS

THE PATH TO PROSPERITY & SUSTAINABILITY

WILEY

Library of Congress Cataloging-in-Publication Data:

Names: Hoffmann, André, author. | Vanham, Peter, 1986- author.
Title: The new nature of business : the path to prosperity and
  sustainability / André Hoffmann, Peter Vanham.
Description: Hoboken, New Jersey : Wiley, [2024] | Includes index.
Identifiers: LCCN 2024020837 (print) | LCCN 2024020838 (ebook) | ISBN
  9781394257539 (hardback) | ISBN 9781394257553 (adobe pdf) | ISBN
  9781394257546 (epub)
Subjects: LCSH: Business. | Sustainability.
Classification: LCC HF1008 .H64 2024 (print) | LCC HF1008 (ebook) | DDC
  658.4/08--dc23/eng/20240601
LC record available at https://lccn.loc.gov/2024020837
LC ebook record available at https://lccn.loc.gov/2024020838

Cover Design: Wiley
Cover Image: © Victor Picon
SKY10079490_080524

(From André) To my wife and all my family.
Long-term thinking is key!

(From Peter) To Valeria, Eloise, and Amélie,
for defining my "new nature" as husband and father.

Contents

Acknowledgments

From André: Thank you to my father for teaching me about natural capital, to my mother for alerting me at an early age about the importance of social capital, and to my wife Rosalie for helping me to build huge stores of human capital. You made me who I am and inspired this book.

Thus equipped I journeyed through life and its many pitfalls and opportunities with a curious and open attitude. I was able to connect with many fascinating people and their opinions. They are probably too many for an exhaustive list. All those aha! moments were inspired by meetings, readings, and events, and I am sure that those who helped me to progress the new nature of business are aware of how they contributed to this book.

I must single out my coauthor Peter. Our sessions and our correspondence about so many aspects of our manuscript have really brought us both much further than I thought possible when we started. Thank you.

The last 20 years of my life have been heavily influenced by my election to the board of Hoffmann La Roche. Fritz Gerber, Franz Humer, Gottlieb Keller, Severin Schwan, and many more were a constant help, as well as my co-board member—and particularly my cousin—Andreas Oeri.

At the same time, I started developing a portfolio of activities both within health care and in other activities. Here as well allow me to single out a couple of individuals. Claude Martin at WWF; Jorgen Randers at WWF and later Fondation du Tour du Valat; Sir John Krebs at Tour du Valat as well, and then Oxford University; Mike Rands at Birdlife International and later Cambridge Conservation Initiative; Gus Christie at Glyndebourne; Klaus Schwab at the World Economic Forum; Robin Niblett at Chatham House; John Chipman at IISS; George Weidenfeld of so many different organizations; Pavan Suhkdev of TEEB and then GIST; Mark Gough of Capitals Coalition; Marco Lambertini from WWF and now the Nature Positive Initiative.

A special mention should be made to INSEAD and to dean Mihov and Veloso. Katell Le Goulven, executive director of the Hoffmann institute, deserves my eternal gratitude for so much talent and energy at the service of both the school and the sustainable prosperity.

Let me also pay homage to my mentors over the years. Dr. A. Rupert, Prof. F. Bourlière, Georges Weidenfeld, and all these people who during one conversation or between two doors have brought me food for thought. My three sisters were particularly good at this, and I thank them for their guidance and challenges over the years.

Finally, none of these would be possible without the support of my office and I am very grateful to Jean, Charlotte, Jakob, and Ilona for their commitment and friendly support. Without them my life would be much more difficult. Jean was instrumental in the development of InTent, one of our more successful initiatives of the last years. Again, thank you to all.

In closing my thanks go to you, our readers. May this book succeed in sharing some of the excitement and sense of purpose that this way of thinking has brought to me.

★ ★ ★

From Peter: Any book has two stories: the one that is printed in ink and the one that is only found in between the lines. The latter, for me, has been one of a small group of people working together and supporting each other for two and a half years—during what for me was without a doubt the most eventful time of my life.

When I first approached André with the idea of writing a book together, I was head of chairman's communications at an international organization, and I lived as a "DINK" (double income, no kids) couple with my wife Valeria in Geneva. As we conclude writing this book, I work as editorial director, leadership, at Fortune Media, and my wife and I have two beautiful daughters, Eloise and Amélie.

So, my gratitude goes out first and foremost to the two people who were the constant human factors in this story: my coauthor André, and my wife Valeria. They were there from the start, every step of the way since, and now as we get ready for launch and promotion.

I wish to thank also those around us who supported us, helped us write, provided their feedback, and gave us the opportunity to publish our book.

Specifically, I wish to thank Alegria and Enrique, my parents-in-law for helping Valeria and me find a balanced way to work and raise our children with love during the most challenging period of our life; the Craen family (Dirk, Carl, Luc, An, and Martine) for their unconditional support in my writing and teaching projects; Alan Murray, Lisa Cline, Jim Jacovides, Mike Kiley, Matt Heimer, and Indrani Sen at Fortune for finding the synergies with the work we do together at Fortune; and Bill Falloon, Susan Cerra, and Purvi Patel at Wiley for being longtime partners in the publishing of our books.

Thank you to Jean and Charlotte in André's office; to all our interviewees and their supporting teams at Roche, ISSB, Holcim, Schneider Electric, Innergia, The B Team, Harley Davidson, IKEA, and INSEAD; and to Rosalie and Frederic, who helped provide ideas, suggested edits, and proofread our manuscript.

Finally: you may not realize it yet, but Eloise and Amélie, you were always on my mind as I worked on this project. Thank you for being such wonderful children and for having joined us on our new nature journey as it crystallized. I hope our efforts may benefit you and your generation, and that you will have found our efforts to define the new nature of business and society useful.

About the Authors

André Hoffmann is a Swiss business leader and environmentalist. He believes in business as a force for good, and advocates for a form of capitalism aimed at generating sustainable and inclusive prosperity.

André is the vice-chair of Roche; a member of the board of governors of the World Economic Forum, and a board member at several other businesses and organizations that promote systems change, regenerative practices, and new norms of corporate leadership, including The B Team, SystemIQ, Landbanking Group, and GIST.

As a fourth-generation family representative at Roche, one of the largest and oldest health care companies in the world, André is a guardian of the company's purpose of "doing now what patients need next." Through his family office, André also makes impact investments in other companies, such as the renewable and locally anchored energy company Innergia.

In addition to his business engagements, André and his wife Rosalie are cofounders of the Hoffmann Institute at INSEAD, the business school of which he is an alum, and InTent, a nonprofit organization that seeks to drive sustainable change in business and society through partnerships between businesses and NGOs.

André is the president of the Fondation Tour du Valat, an institute dedicated to wetlands conservation, and previously served as vice-chair of the World Wide Fund for Nature (WWF). André studied economics at St. Gallen University and holds an MBA from INSEAD. He and his wife live and work near Lake Geneva, Switzerland.

★ ★ ★

Peter Vanham is a Belgian business journalist and author who writes about the global economy and the people who shape it, and focuses on stakeholder capitalism and sustainability.

As an author, his books include *Stakeholder Capitalism: A Global Economy that Works for Progress, People and Planet* (with Klaus Schwab, 2021) and *Before I Was CEO: Life Stories and Lessons from Leaders Before They Reached the Top* (2016). His books have been translated in more than a dozen languages.

As a journalist, Peter currently serves as editorial director, leadership, at *Fortune*, where he is also the coauthor of *CEO Daily*. Prior to that, he was head writer and head of the International Media Council at the World Economic Forum. His articles appeared in dozens of global media, including *Financial Times*, *Harvard Business Review*, and *Foreign Policy*.

Peter holds executive master's degrees in management research (ESCP) and global leadership (World Economic Forum), and master's degrees in business and economics journalism (Columbia University) and commercial engineering (KU Leuven). He lives and works in Geneva, Switzerland, with his wife and two daughters.

Introduction

It was a rainy afternoon back in 2003, when I got the phone call that could have been the beginning of the end of my family's then 107-year-old company. "You must come to Basel immediately," the man on the other side of the line said. "Come to my private home."

Alarmed, I got into my car, typed in the address in what was then still a brand-new technology—the GPS navigation system—and . . . almost got lost. (GPS navigation wasn't as smooth and reliable as it is today!) The device instructed me from my home through the forested back roads of Switzerland to the northern border city of Basel, just as a heavy rain poured down. It was like being in a movie.

When I finally got to my destination, I got the news. "We have just received a call from Novartis," Fritz Gerber, the then-chairman of our family company, Roche, and a confidant of my family, told me. "They are interested in acquiring the family shares."

This chapter is written in André's voice.

I hadn't been expecting that message. Over the course of more than 100 years, my great-grandfather Fritz Hoffmann and his descendants helped grow Roche from an experimental pharmaceutical start-up into the global pharma leader it was when I joined the board in the mid-1990s. Roche had been among the largest pharmaceutical companies in the world for most of its existence. It certainly was one of the world's largest family-controlled companies. And it had never been any generation's intention to change that legacy.

We had seen ups and downs, both in the company's fate and that of our family. Nevertheless, the company had created value in the long run, and had a symbiotic relationship with our hometown of Basel, the country, and the health industry at large. We had also managed to hold on to the majority of voting shares in our company, even as our overall shareholding had diluted, as 20th-century history affected us and our company. Now, a large minority shareholder had just sold its voting shares to Novartis.

★ ★ ★

As I let the news sink in, my mind went to what a potential merger would mean for others. What good would it bring to Basel, Switzerland, the pharma industry, or the economy at large? Novartis was our neighbor across the Rhine. It was itself the result of a merger of two 19th-century competitors of ours—Sandoz and Ciba Geigy. I respected the company as one that kept us always alert. They were a constant reminder that in a free-market innovation and competition are crucial to survive. But it was never anyone's intention in the family to merge, and we weren't alone in seeing things that way. "Bread is better in a town with two bakers," one of our new top executives would say. The merged company would lead to market concentration certainly in Basel and Switzerland, and to a certain extent the global pharmaceutical industry as well. It would bring a lot of social disturbance to the combined company—and it wasn't certain it would be better for other stakeholders, either.

Still, we faced a difficult decision. Although the resulting company would bring an end to our ownership, it would also enable the merged company to take a fresh start. As a family, we had taken a hands-off approach to Roche's ownership for decades, mostly since my grandfather's untimely death in a car accident in the 1930s. Entrusting the company's day-to-day management to nonfamily members worked well for a long time, but cracks had started to appear. Just a few years earlier, our company had gotten in trouble, being convicted in the US after a vitamin price-fixing scandal. Roche was obliged to pay a multibillion-dollar fine. And all of us with ties to the company had had to accept that this had happened under our watch. The fact that as owners, we had been ignorant about such practices and failed to prevent them from happening, had sown doubt even among ourselves about our ability to steer the company into the 21st century. Wouldn't everyone be better off with the proposed merger, after all?

As I drove back in the middle of the night from Basel, those conflicting thoughts were on my mind. As one of only two family members on the board, many of my relatives would look to me to come up with a first reaction. And I had to admit: If someone made an offer for the entirety of our company, it was probably because the company was undervalued. We—and I—needed to think hard about what our added value as family owners was.

We also had to answer the imminent question in front of us: Do we go to the "safe" route of cashing in, and allow the two industrial assets to merge? Or are we willing to fight on our own, with a lower financial return in the short term, perhaps, but potentially also a better long-term outcome for shareholders *and* stakeholders?

★ ★ ★

Today, as I think back of those events two decades ago, I realize that in that moment of crisis also lay the start of my vision for our company and the role of business in society more broadly.

We did in fact maintain our independence, and built the Roche of the 21st century, following the north star of "doing now what the patient needs next." Product-wise, drugs like Tamiflu and several of our oncology drugs became big successes in the years following the takeover bid, helping millions of people, and proving the value of the raison d'être of our company to patients. They also proved to be a financial vindication of our approach, as Roche surpassed Novartis in market capitalization in the 2010s, after trailing it at the time of the bid.

Before we got there, though, there had been many things to sort out, including about our *purpose*. I had had to define for myself and my family members what my proposed alternative to a merger would look like—and why it was better. As I had mulled this over, my basic belief had come to be this: A company does not exist *solely* to make money for its shareholders in the short term. Novartis, Roche, or any other company should not simply aim to maximize profits or "total shareholder returns" in the next quarter or year. Of course, from the narrowly defined view on "fiduciary duty," any well-meaning advisor would have been excused to tell my family at the time—or any shareholder of a takeover target—it was better to sell. But it would not have advanced what I now see as the central responsibility of a company and those who own it: to create sustainable and inclusive prosperity. The new nature of business, I came to believe, had to include adding value to society, and doing so in an inclusive way that doesn't harm the environment.

Why do I want to tell this story, and that of my journey? Because after many decades of peace and prosperity, the societies we are part of are faced with turmoil, and even existential threats. Just as my family members and I were at a crossroads 20 years ago (or Roche's previous stewards were in the turbulent first half of the 20th century), I feel like all of us are today. In my family, a new generation is getting ready to steer business and the economy into a new direction. The narrow context in which my children and their cousins will need to reinvent the family business is one where new Roche products and offerings need to be brought to market, as a previous generation of "blockbusters" loses steam. But the next generation also needs to reinvent the business model in a broader context, where no business can be unsustainable any longer in the environmental and societal sense. Businesses need to be regenerative, adding more to society and the planet than they take from it, whether from a natural resource, financial, human, or societal perspective.

Collectively, we haven't yet figured out how to meet that challenge, and time is running out. Will we continue to think and act in the short term and in our narrow self-interest, or will take a more enlightened approach? As you—the current and next generation—tackle this question, I hope you can build on the insights I gained throughout the years of stewarding Roche.

★ ★ ★

Of course, companies and their owners, management, and employees cannot solve all the multitude of crises we are facing today—at least not alone. But by taking our responsibility, we sure can do more than they are doing today in creating the sustainable and inclusive prosperity we so badly need. Today's economic actors still destroy more value than they create, mostly because they don't account for the natural, social, and human externalities they bring about. That upsets me, as it means we are sleepwalking toward more disasters in the future.

But at the same time, I'm not a doomsday thinker. My frustrations lead me neither to despair nor a blanket *j'accuse* toward my peers. I do not believe we are helpless in the face of the crises we are confronted with. I also do not believe we need an actual *revolution* to turn things around. (My mother's family was dispossessed of their estates in Central Europe, after a revolution brought the communists to power there. They would not forgive me for such failure to learn from history.) In fact, besides being an environmentalist I am also a capitalist, and I believe capitalism can provide the answers to the challenges we are facing.

As vice-chairman of a family-controlled company, the prosperity I enjoy came about because of private ownership, free trade, competition, and innovation our company could benefit from. At the same token, the society I am part of benefited from our family company's entrepreneurship as well. Basel today is the prosperous town it is, thanks in large part to the business leaders who shaped the city throughout the centuries, building industries that brought employment and welfare to the entire region. At a global level, the pharmaceutical innovations launched by Roche and other similar enterprises improved the lives of most people with access to health care today. So, I believe it is for good reason that my family has fought to preserve our Roche ownership rights over generations: long-term stewardship of assets can lead to long-term investments, innovation, and improvements, and help lift entire communities.

I do, however, also believe we require collectively a more enlightened approach to capitalism. The reason is that prosperity isn't created by the *financial capital* of individual entrepreneurs alone. It is also the result of *social, natural,* and *human capital* that is found and built throughout society and our planet. If we want to preserve our system of democratic capitalism, we need to ensure our system is sustainable in the long run and beneficial for everybody. That is not (only) a moral imperative; it is a matter of the system's long-term survival, and it is an underpinning of the democratic side of capitalism.

In this book, my coauthor Peter and I present some of the concepts and cases I've reflected on in the past 20 years as I sought to build the stepping stones of a more sustainable and inclusive economic system. Some of them have been applied at Roche as it charted its way after the takeover bid. Other examples come from some other companies and leaders I have come to know and appreciate. And yet others are at a more experimental stage, with widespread implementation still (and hopefully soon) to follow. I recognize fully that they do not add up to a full solution. Nor do I miss the irony of a billionaire writing about equity and sustainability. But we need all hands on deck to build a more sustainable future, and this is my attempted contribution.

In writing this book, I draw on my own experience, and that of our family business. I share personal anecdotes and past company stories that I hope may inspire you, either because they show success or enable learning from failure. And I look to the present and future, presenting both ideas and practices that I believe will help us all to build sustainable, inclusive prosperity going forward. These are challenges I hope to help address, but that will mostly be solved—or not—by those that come after me: my children and all their fellow young people around the world. I hope this book may be a help to them (and to you!), either because it helps change the ways of those in establishment today or because it encourages those who will soon succeed us. I wish you all an inspiring read.

Chapter 1

The Myth of the Founder and a Company's Capitals

My great-grandfather, Fritz Hoffmann-La Roche, was a visionary entrepreneur. From 1896, he pioneered the nascent pharmaceutical industry, overcoming countless hurdles and challenges. He even nearly went bankrupt. But by the time he died, he had built a multinational corporation that still operates today as one of the largest and most impactful pharmaceutical companies in the world.

I love to look back on this story. And yet there's a problem with it. This story is too much centered on the achievements of one person.

We often hear business success is the result of individual genius, entrepreneurship, and persistence. We are told that founders are a special breed, and different from us. That they see solutions where others see obstacles. That they see the future, where we can only see the present. And that they succeed, not because of circumstances,

---

This chapter is written in André's voice.

but because they are destined to win and do what it takes to fulfill this destiny.

We know this myth not just from my great-grandfather but also from some of the world's richest men of today, such as Elon Musk, Bill Gates, and other Silicon Valley billionaires. Musk cofounded PayPal, predicting the future of online payments. He also cofounded the electric vehicle pioneer Tesla and turned it into the most valuable car company in the world. And he continues his entrepreneurial ventures today with companies such as SpaceX, Neuralink, and xAI, pioneering everything from space industry to artificial intelligence (AI). Gates brought modern computing to the masses, popularizing PCs through Microsoft's Windows and Office software. Both built business empires that advanced human progress and propelled societies forward.

But these mythologies, just like my great-grandfather's, are misleading. Not factually, but they miss the bigger picture.

Fritz Hoffmann-La Roche was exactly as I just described. But he was also a child of his time and the world around him. To succeed, he could bank on several "capitals" that were uniquely available to him. These included the financial capital, which was given to him by his father, father-in-law, and other family members and associates. And they included social, natural, and human capital, all available in Basel, the city on the Rhine River where Fritz was born and spent almost his entire life.

This chapter is about these capitals. We will explore their role in conjunction with the success of Roche, the company in which my family has a controlling share to the present day. And we will show how they are just as relevant for us in today's and tomorrow's capitalism as in that of Fritz and his family at the end of the 19th century.

Financial Capital

It's hard to understate the importance of financial capital, yet easy to overlook it. My great-grandfather, who was born in 1868, was fortunate to have access to financial capital at a time where only a few people had the opportunity. When he came of age, new companies using chemical and pharmaceutical processes started to emerge in the city. And in 1893, he joined one such company, Bohny, Hollinger & Cie, which produced flooring wax and soap in the city, which operated a department store with some nascent pharmaceutical offerings.

As Fritz gained experience in the company, his vision started to develop: if a company could industrialize the production of sanitary and pharmaceutical products, he figured, it could supply drug stores everywhere, and become as successful as any other industrial company. But to get there, he needed a lot of things to come together. The first thing, of course, was money. Thanks to his father, Friedrich, a successful businessman, that was not an insurmountable challenge. His father soon invested the substantial sum of 200,000 Swiss Francs into Bohny, Hollinger & Cie, and Fritz was subsequently promoted, becoming an authorized representative of the company.[a]

The idea of pioneering the pharmaceutical industry was a promising, if risky one. By the time my great-grandfather entered the scene, industrialists were already successful in heavy industries like steel or coal, railroads, and textile. Once a successful industrial process was identified, the way to success was well-defined: you invested the capital necessary to build a factory, and from there, the rest followed; you installed novel machinery, hired personnel, bought commodity inputs in bulk, and finally, sold the industrial products in newly established markets. It was the recipe of industrialists such as Robert Owen (textile, UK), Andrew Carnegie (steel, US) or Ernest Solvay (chemicals, Belgium).

Pharmaceutical products, though, were still largely made in artisanal pharmacies, with a local pharmacist concocting the

---

[a] Technically, Fritz received power of attorney, meaning he had the legal right to represent the company, for example, by signing contracts on behalf of the firm.

different products their pharmacy offered. But Fritz had an inkling this sector, too, was ripe for industrialization.

Just as important as having capital, though, is maintaining your access to it. That was as true in the late 1890s as it is today. Fritz was confronted with this timeless reality sooner than perhaps he wanted to. He soon fell out with his conservative partners in the business who disliked his modern style and saw himself forced to either double down on his prior investment and take over the whole company or write off the loss. With the financial help of his father and the company's factory head, Max Carl Traub, he was able to choose the first route. They founded the new company Hoffmann, Traub & Co. on April 2, 1894.

The idea of creating industrialized pharmaceuticals may have been a good one, but it was not as easy to make it work at the time. The company's first product, a wound disinfectant called Airol, did not sell well at first.[b] But instead of giving up, Fritz powered through. He set up shop in Milan in 1895 and started to buy land and build a purpose-built pharmaceutical plant in Grenzach (Germany) from May 1896 onwards. At that point, however, his business partner Traub wanted out. He thought the quick expansion of the company—which was not based on any proper income through sales—was a huge risk to his investment. He asked Fritz Hoffmann-La Roche to pay his stake off. Once more, Fritz could do so only with the (now very reluctant) financial help of his father in September 1896, and the company F. Hoffmann-La Roche & Co. was registered on October 1, 1896. (Fritz had married Adèle La Roche by now, and added her name to his, resulting in the Hoffmann-La Roche company name.)

Personal persistence and pharmaceutical breakthroughs would help him as well in the years to come, but it was the financial capital his family backers provided which kept Fritz in business. And it ultimately paid off. By 1898, the F. Hoffmann-La Roche

---

[b] It did become very successful in Russia in a later point in time as Alexander Bieri, Roche's historian, pointed out.

company put its first successful pharmaceutical product onto the market: Sirolin, a cough syrup that contained an active ingredient called *thiocol*. It was sold for over half a century and constituted the first true global "blockbuster" for the firm. At the eve of World War I, before the company even celebrated its 20th anniversary, sirolin and other novel "Roche" medicines were sold everywhere from Paris to St. Petersburg, and from Yokohama to New York. (Over time, F. Hoffmann–La Roche started to use the name *Roche* for short, primarily because it found this part of the name the one that translated best to other languages and countries.)

When recounting the story of successful founders and companies, we tend to brush over fundraising as if it comes naturally. But as this little story suggests, financial capital is not available to everyone. Getting access to it depends as much on one's network as on one's business ideas. It makes the responsibility of those who have it crucial. Deploying financial capital for one venture or another helps set the course of history of entire communities, cities, and society at large. The story of Roche is a good historical example, but there are just as many in the present day. Indeed, financial capital has played just as big of a role for the most successful entrepreneurs of recent times. Consider the stories from Apple, Amazon, Google, and Meta.

Many people are familiar with the legend of Apple: college dropouts Steve Jobs and Steve Wozniak founded Apple back in 1976[1] in Wozniak's garage in Silicon Valley. But within a year, Jobs realized that the company needed funding to grow. At that time, it was former Intel employee Mark Markkula who put in a significant amount of money and became Apple's largest shareholder.[2]

Similarly, when Jeff Bezos started Amazon in 1994, he immediately looked for seed funding. Just like with many other entrepreneurs, it came from his parents. They provided Bezos with $300,000,[3] enough to keep the company going until a second round raised $8 million from venture capital fund Kleiner Perkins in 1995.[4] As for Google founders Sergey Brin and Larry Page, they had been tinkering around with a search engine at Stanford since 1995. But Google Inc. only came into being as such, after a $100,000 investment by Sun Microsystems founder Andy Bechtolsheim in 1998.[5]

Finally, Meta, the company Mark Zuckerberg among others founded as Thefacebook.com in early 2004, received its first funding of $500,000 barely three months after its incorporation in a Harvard dorm room, and less than a year after the project was conceived. The money came from PayPal cofounder and venture capital investor Peter Thiel.[6] And speaking of PayPal founders: Elon Musk, who now is mostly known for Tesla, SpaceX, and X, started out as an entrepreneur founding Zip2, an internet 1.0 business search company. He may have got closest to bootstrapping, starting out with only $15,000 in its initial funding round, of which just under half came from himself and his brother. Even so, the majority investment in that first funding round, came from a third party: Greg Kouri,[7] a Lebanese American businessman who also joined Zip2 in an operational role early on.

This is not to take away anything from the achievements of these incredible entrepreneurs. But it bears repeating: the financial capital these companies received at the time of their inception and in the immediate years following was crucial to their success. Without it, the great innovations these men created for the world, may have come to nothing. This matters, because what is true for the world's largest technology and pharmaceutical companies is also true for companies working on technology, sustainability, or climate today. Creating a sustainable *and* prosperous economic system is the great and unmet challenge of the 21st century. We'll need visionary entrepreneurs to create companies that rise to that challenge, just as we had entrepreneurs rising to the challenges and opportunities of the internet era of Bezos and Gates, or the industrialization era of my great-grandfather. But we'll also need funders to provide these entrepreneurs with the financial capital they need. For many among them, finding the right capital has been perhaps their greatest hurdle.

So how do you get access to financial capital?

Social Capital

If my great-grandfather was able to fund his innovative start-up back in the 1890s, it was primarily because his father and father-in-law had the financial means to do so. But that immediately raises a second question: where did *their* money come from? There is a narrow answer to this question, of course, which it is that both men had successful businesses themselves. But the longer answer is that they were both members of the *Daig* families that controlled much of Basel's economic development since medieval times. Like other leading families, the Hoffmann's and La Roche's got their capital by building out the silk industry in the city. Both families played their individual roles, leading companies and taking up posts as mayors or aldermen. But taken together, the families were an important constituent of Basel's social capital.

Social capital is more intangible than financial capital, but just as important in building successful ventures. According to *Britannica*, it consists of three dimensions: the interconnected networks of relationships between individuals and groups, the levels of trust that characterize these ties, and the resources or benefits that are both gained and transferred by virtue of social ties and social participation.[8] Fritz was at the receiving end of centuries of this kind of social capital accumulation in the city of Basel, which had started in medieval times. As people moved to emerging urban centers, they provided their host cities with an invisible, yet powerful engine of development. In the case of Basel, immigrants imported knowledge from elsewhere, such as the silk industry in Northern Italy and southern France. They got attracted by the city's religious liberty, and its relative autonomy from lords and bishops. Their entrepreneurial drive turned the city on the Rhine into a prosperous industrial and commercial center. There was a network of free citizens and artisans within the city walls, and trust among them. And as this process accelerated, these entrepreneurs also secured a leading role for themselves in the city's political and economic life. The leading families among them became known as the *Daig*.

As elsewhere, events of the 19th century disrupted the status quo in Basel. The revolutionary spirit that came from nearby France led the citizens of Basel's countryside to demand self-rule from the city. It led to a political division still in place today, with the historical Canton of Basel split into Basel-City ("Basel-City"), and Basel-Landschaft ("Basel-Countryside"). But the changes weren't only political. Newcomers from outside Basel and Switzerland moved to the city to start up new businesses, too, notably in the chemical industry. It led, over time, to the decline of the silk industry, and the rise of a new one. My great-grandfather and his family embodied continuity amid this turmoil. With the creation of F. Hoffmann-La Roche, they helped Basel into the next golden era built on pharmaceutical and chemical prowess—one that would go on to sustain itself until today. But if they succeeded in this transformation, it was in large part thanks to the city's social capital. Fritz could acquire land near the city, hire both skilled and unskilled labor, and insert his new company in the trade and finance links the city had with the outside world, thanks to the social capital present in the city and his access to it.

Today's leading entrepreneurs built their success in a similar way. They had access to similar networks and lived and worked in regions with an abundance of social capital.

The founders of Apple, for example, could lean on a former Intel employee for their seed capital, and took a page from a nearby company—Hewlett Packard—to start up their company from a garage. At Google, Larry Page and Sergey Brin stormed the tech scene in the 1990s, after having had their beginnings in Stanford University. That both these trillion-dollar companies started in the Bay Area, was by no means a coincidence. Already by the 1960s, *Silicon Valley*, as the area was also known, had emerged as the world's leading center for computer technology and venture capital. Its social capital included university researchers and their innovations, such as Stanford; military bases and their contractors based around San Francisco; the region's history of entrepreneurship, including tech pioneers such as Bill Hewlett and David Packard (who started out in 1939); and an openness to immigrants from around the world, including Asia. Apple and Google's founders may have become the poster boys of Silicon Valley, but they didn't create it.

Many entrepreneurs explicitly seek out regions with high social capital to succeed. Mark Zuckerberg may be unique in combining two such places. You could argue that Facebook's core strength wasn't so much its technological innovation, but the social capital it was built on, both as a company and as a social network. Other companies had built similar features to their websites and become initially more successful. But Facebook had something its competitors did not have: its network was made up of Harvard students, allowing it to lean on the social capital of the university. Having high-profile and well-connected students as first users, Facebook first expanded to other renowned US university campuses, and then internationally and across the US from there. Then, to become the company Meta is today, Zuckerberg also tapped into the social capital of Silicon Valley. According to Scott Kirstner, a journalist of the *Boston Globe*, Zuckerberg moved to Palo Alto after Peter Thiel, one of the founders of Silicon Valley–based PayPal, invested in his company when others in Boston would not.[9] And it wasn't just Thiel's money that made the company so successful afterwards. "So many of the Facebook employees have come from top Internet companies like Yahoo, eBay, and Google that the culture that has been built at Facebook is fundamentally more consumer Internet savvy than if it would've been built anywhere else on the planet," Jim Breyer, a partner at VC firm Accel, told Kirstner back in 2007.[10]

A similar tale played out about 800 miles north of San Francisco, in Seattle. Many people know part of the origin story of Microsoft: how Bill Gates and Paul Allen met in a Seattle high school; how they got passionate about the one computer the school had, and, how as college students, they created a software system to make computers, such as those of market leader IBM, yet more user-friendly.[11] The rest of the story is history. But when you pick each of the foundational elements of Microsoft's founding apart, you see how they're all enabled by social capital. To begin with, it was one Lakeside high school teacher, Bill Dougall, who wanted his students to have access to a computer terminal, Paul Allen later recalled.[12] Dougall approached the Lakeside Mothers Club for the endeavor, and they "agreed to use the proceeds from [their] annual rummage sale to lease a teleprinter terminal for computer time-sharing." Allen and Gates were among the computer's most avid users, thanks to the open-minded Lakeside teachers, and the forward-thinking, well-off Lakeside mothers. "They could have hired an outside computer expert to do the scheduling system," Gates later said.[13] "Teachers could have insisted that they teach classes on computing, simply because they were the teachers, and we were the students. But they didn't. If there had been no Lakeside, there would have been no Microsoft."

In the years following, Allen and Gates went ever further in pursuing their love for computer programming, and Seattle's social capital allowed for it. While they were still in high school, Paul Gilbert, a college student at the University of Washington, helped the two get access to the university's Sigma mainframe computer, which was more powerful than the Lakeside one, and could be used for data processing, Allen recalled.[14] "If not for all the time [we] spent on UW computers, you could argue that Microsoft might not have happened," Allen told the university back in 2017. Finally, it was Gates's mother who introduced the two to John Opel, the then-chairman of IBM.[15] Both Gates's parents were active in Seattle's King County chapter of United Way, a nonprofit, and it was here that Mary Gates met Opel, who was also on the organization's board. From Lakeside high school to the University of Washington to United Way: all these organizations were part of the social fabric that Allen and Gates tapped into on their way to founding Microsoft.

Many years later, as Jeff Bezos was considering where best to build Amazon, Seattle had already been transformed by Microsoft's presence. It was because of Microsoft's role in making Seattle a tech hub, then, that Bezos decided he would set up shop there.

Brad Stone, a journalist who wrote the book *The Everything Store: Jeff Bezos and the Age of Amazon*, added an interesting detail to that social capital story: "Bezos chose to start his company in Seattle," he wrote, "because of the city's reputation as a technology hub and because the state of Washington had a relatively small population [. . .] which meant that Amazon would have to collect state sales tax from only a minor percentage of customers. While the area was still a remote urban outpost known more for its grunge rock than its business community, Microsoft was hitting its stride in nearby Redmond, and the University of Washington produced a steady stream of computer science graduates."[16]

Natural Capital

Natural capital is the next building block for many successful companies. It arises when people can turn the natural environment they encounter into an asset, or into an input for their business. That happens in a variety of ways and benefits companies both directly and indirectly. Let's take a look at Roche.

Borders, especially natural ones like mountain tops or rivers, can be very limiting. They keep people from crossing them because of the dangers they pose, separating communities from another. But borders can also be inviting. They can bring people together when humans find out how to cross and bridge them, turning obstacles into connection points.

Basel represents both these types of borders. It is built on a crucial junction of the Rhine, one of the longest and widest rivers on the European continent. For millennia, the river was a symbol of the power of nature over man, because it was so hard to cross. (In fact, even today, the river is a natural border among France, Germany, and Switzerland, a division that started millennia ago.) But starting in Roman times, people also started to see how they could bridge the river, literally. And they learned to use the river's strength—its impressive length and current—to their benefit. As humans learned to master the river, the Rhine became the vein through which European economic life flowed. It became the longest navigable river in Europe, and the one carrying the lion's share of the region's trade. The cities along the Rhine, from Rotterdam in the Rhine's delta; over Duisburg, Dusseldorf, Cologne, Bonn, Mainz, and Mannheim in Germany; and Strasbourg in France, are still today among the most populated and prosperous ones in Europe, benefiting from the Rhine's natural riches.

The same applies to Basel. The Swiss border city lies hundreds of kilometers upstream to the Rhine, closer to its source than its delta, and at a double crossroads. It is here where some of Europe's most impenetrable natural borders meet, and the Rhine takes a 90-degree turn toward the more open lands that follow. To its southwest are the Jura mountains, separating Switzerland from France. To its northeast is Germany's Black Forest, which has always fascinated and frightened those who journeyed in it and remains to this day a barrier between Germany and its neighbors. Basel, then, was a meeting point: one between France and Germany, with which it both shares a border. And one between Switzerland and the river road to the sea. For centuries, it had the only permanent bridge over the Rhine, connecting not just two of its city neighborhoods, but the wider world around it.

It is this natural capital that made Basel into the crossroads it was when my great-grandfather was born there: a city where merchants, researchers, and immigrants from all of Europe had been meeting for centuries, and where some of them had stayed and contributed to the city as it developed. As early as the Renaissance, thinkers such as Erasmus of Rotterdam had come here because of the city's welcoming climate for free thinkers, but also its blossoming printing and paper industries, enabled by the city's abundant river water. In the 19th century, the Rhine played a similar enabling role for the chemical industry and indeed the pharmaceutical industry. The Rhine allowed for the easy import of inputs. It played a role in the processing and production of industrial goods. And it transported finished goods back out of the city and to Europe and the world.

But natural capital isn't only about geography. In many companies, Roche included, the most important natural capital is the natural inputs that go into their products (a company's nature-related "dependencies") and the effect their sold products have on the environment (nature-related "impacts").

One example clarifies the dependency side: Tamiflu, an antiviral medicine to treat the flu and other influenza viruses. Roche has been producing Tamiflu since the late 1990s, helping patients and public health systems around the world, and generating billions of dollars in sales.[17] At the origin of Tamiflu of course lies a multimillion-dollar R&D effort, led by excellent scientists, in this case from Roche's US partner Gilead Sciences. But Tamiflu also has a very natural key ingredient: shikimic acid,[18] harvested from the star anise flower, native to Vietnam and Southern China. The same is true for many other drugs and medicinal products, and not just herbal ones. Nature is a crucial building block, or dependency, for virtually any company. Even the world's most valuable company in 2024, Nvidia, could not make what it sells without silica, glass, aluminum, and copper,[19] to name just a few of the inputs that go into its powerful GPU processors which power the most hyped technology of our time: AI.

For other companies, the reliance on natural capital is even more clear-cut than is the case for Roche or Nvidia. Basic industries such as mining, oil, and gas, are explicitly dependent on the natural capital of the place they own or operate. The same is true for the agricultural, food, or chemical industries, and so many others. The historical modus operandi for obtaining natural resources in many primary industries is straightforward, if flawed. The governments that most often own the mines, sources, or fields these companies operate in, put a price tag on the commercial exploitation of their natural resources, either handing a concession to the highest bidder or selling the properties outright. It has been a common practice since at least medieval times, and it has worked well—economic development wouldn't have been possible without it. But the method is also flawed, because it is based primarily on the price these resources fetch in the market. In most cases, these contracts do not adequately account for the negative externalities the exploited resources cause at the time of use, nor those that emerge from their extraction itself, nor any impacts their exploitation will have on future generations.

By now the point should be clear: when we pay attention to it, we see that natural capital is omnipresent in any company's history and present, and indeed, in the global economy at large. The British journalist Ed Conway put it well in his 2023 book *Material World: The Six Raw Materials That Shape Modern Civilization*[20]: "While terms like the Stone, Bronze, and the Iron Age are typically used to refer to distant, forgotten eras," he wrote, "Actually our reliance on physical tools and materials has exploded rather than is diminishing. Given how much sand and rock we still blast from the planet, we are still firmly embedded in the Stone Age. Our need for steel and copper has multiplied in recent years. This then, is also the Iron Age, not to mention the age of copper, of salt, of oil and lithium." Without these natural resources, Conway continues, "we might, just about, be able to live . . . but we could not thrive without them . . . They helped us build our world, and we would be thrown in chaos if we were to lose access to them."

On the other side of the equation are a company's impacts on nature. They are often not all that positive. Roche is, historically speaking, no exception. A study the company's management commissioned a few years back found that the "impact costs at the Swiss sites compared with Swiss revenues were found to be in the order of 6% of net sales."[21] It is a relatively low cost, the then assessor, the Natural Capitals Coalition, said, but its greenhouse gas emissions and water use still lead to negative impacts (The Natural Capitals Coalition today continues its work as simply the "Capitals Coalition," after having merged with an organization studying social and human capital.)

Another historical example further highlights that companies, Roche included, can have a very negative impact on nature when they ignore the impacts of their operations. When Roche was still active in the chemical industry, in the 1950s and 1960s, notably, it used the Rhine and its riverbed as an open sewer, and a landfill for waste. So did many other chemical companies in the region. Managers of the plants at first didn't know any better. Dropping waste in a landfill or into the water had been a practice for decades, if not centuries. And even when the harmful effects of their activities became apparent, companies still did not do anything about it. There was no alternative, it was believed. It was generally accepted that industrial waste was an unpleasant but necessary side effect of industrialization, and the progress, jobs, and wealth it generated. But the environment did pay a hefty price, both immediately—with the Rhine's water quality—and in the long term—through the hazard posed by the open-air landfills along the Rhine. By the turn of the 21st century, waste production had long stopped. But the question of what to do with the landfills of the past remained. I'll write more about that in Chapter 7.

Going forward, however, companies will need to be much more aware of the natural capital they are built on and help preserve it. That is because their—and our—prosperity depends on it.

The Hidden Natural Capital of US Big Tech

Natural capital is an indirect or latent asset that benefits a company in myriad ways. America's tech hubs are perfect examples.

It's often forgotten, but the US military presence in Silicon Valley and Seattle is one reason the tech industry took off there. "Defense contracts during and after World War II turned Silicon Valley from a somnolent landscape of fruit orchards into a hub of electronics production and innovations ranging from mainframes to microprocessors to the internet," historian Margaret O'Mara pointed out in a New York Times *commentary in 2018.[22] It means that "the*

(continued)

(continued)

American tech economy rests on the foundations of the military-industrial complex," and that "whether their employees realize it or not, today's tech giants all contain some defense-industry DNA."

But what does that have to do with natural capital? Everything. From the early 20th century, the US Navy had several bases and a shipyard in or near San Francisco. Seattle similarly was home to a large naval base. The reason for these choices was obvious: there were natural harbors giving access to the Pacific, hilltops overseeing land and sea, and, in the case of Seattle, timber, used in all kinds of construction, including that of ships.

Once the military settled on America's West Coast cities, however, it led to a whole set of side effects and spin-offs. Prime among them was ARPAnet, a military computer network developed in the 1950s and 1960s in California.[23] The idea of ARPAnet was to have computers communicate with one another from coast to coast—it was the original concept of what would later become the internet. More broadly, the army's contracts spurred innovation and benefited the regions' entire ecosystem, in both big ways and small. ARPAnet, for example, was developed at Stanford, giving researchers and the institution itself the chance to play a leading role in computer technology. The military's orders of microprocessors gave companies such as Intel the space to grow. And remember Bill Gates and Paul Allen's teacher, Bill Dougal? He was a veteran navy pilot, who had served in Seattle's naval base. The tie-ins also continue until the present day. The military is still one of the largest clients of not just Microsoft, but also Elon Musk's SpaceX, Page and Brin's Google, and the other big tech companies mentioned previously.[24]

As said, the role of natural capital in developing the tech industry is indirect. There is nothing as such about the shape of the San Francisco or Seattle bays—or any other natural capital of the regions, *for that matter—that made them, and not another place, a better breeding ground for tech start-ups. (As an aside: Silicon Valley does get its name from a natural resource: the silicon that is used in the computer chips that many Silicon Valley companies once produced. But this silicon was sourced from a variety of places around the world, not just the San Francisco Bay Area. It is one of the most abundant materials present in the earth's crust.) But you do need to know about the regions' natural capital, because it played a critical role in other industries present there. Without them, Silicon Valley would likely not have existed in the way we know it today. It explains why efforts to create the next Silicon Valley elsewhere often amount to nothing—if they lack a powerful government industry backing them up.*

Human Capital

Finally, we need to account for human capital. The financial, social, and natural capital my great-grandfather could count on explain why he was able to create Roche. But they cannot explain how the company got through the many existential crises it faced in the first 50 years after its founding. To understand how the company got through these ups and downs requires understanding Roche's human capital.

Human capital is about the individual talents and skills of the people that work in your organization. It is about a great manager, an inventive researcher, a talented sales representative, a factory worker with an eye for detail. My great-grandfather, and every generation of owners of Roche since, could count on each one of those, and more.

From the very start of Roche, Fritz understood the importance of human capital. According to Roche's company historian,

Alexander Bieri, Fritz was an "exceedingly modern man when it came to what today would be called 'diversity.'" He hired people from other countries and religions, like his longtime deputy Carl Meerwein (a Dutchman), the Jewish scientist Markus Guggenheim, Roche's first proper head of research, and, later, many Russians who fled their country's revolution in the chaotic last days of the Russian Empire. Most important, perhaps, in 1896 Fritz hired the young chemist Emil Barell, the Catholic son of a poor carpenter from Piedmont who emigrated to Switzerland. Such a hire would probably not occur anywhere else in a Protestant city like Basel, Bieri noted. But this focus on talent, whatever their background, proved to be a recipe for success, literally. It was Barell, notably, who came up with the active ingredients and recipes for many of Roche's early drugs, including the heart medication Digalen (introduced in 1903)[25] and the painkiller Pantopon (launched in 1909). Nor did Barell's impact stop on the product side.

The first World War constituted a major challenge for Roche because several of its key markets, including the Russian, German, and the Austro-Hungarian Empires, collapsed politically, economically, or both. The October Revolution was a particularly bitter pill for Roche, so to speak, because the Russian Empire had been its single largest market until then. With the arrival of the Soviets, Roche's presence was all but wiped out. To make matters worse, Fritz Hoffmann got ill shortly after, and died in 1920. The company's future had never looked so bleak. My great-grandfather's premature death at age 51 came at a time that his sons, Emmanuel, my grandfather, and Alfred, were too young to take over. So, it was Emil Barell, Roche's trusted scientist, who stepped up. He navigated the company through what were perhaps the three most turbulent decades of its history. He recovered some key markets in the 1920s, including Germany, and introduced yet more successful drugs such as the sedative Allonal (launched in 1921), and

Prostigmin (which is still on the list of World Health Organization essential medicines today[26]). But even with those achievements under the belt, Barell faced yet another set of existential challenges in the decades that followed.

To begin with, Fritz's son Emanuel, my grandfather, who had been working at Roche's Brussels office, died in a car crash in 1932, at only 36 years of age. His son, Luc, my father, was barely 9 years old at the time, meaning that the family stewardship of Roche hung by a thread. Second, Roche's main production site, just across the German border from Basel, became increasingly difficult to operate after members of the _Nationalsozialistiche Deutsche Arbeiterpartei_ (the Nazis, for short) of Adolf Hitler came to power in 1933. The Nazi government froze the assets of foreign companies, for example, and restricted exports. That made it hard for Roche, which thrived thanks to exports of products and imports of raw materials, to operate in Germany. The Nazis also politicized how companies were run, enforcing Hitler salutes, among other decisions. In that context, Roche was seen by the Nazis as having a "Jewish problem" because the company had Jewish members on its board of directors, and as several senior managers, including Barell, were married to Jewish women.[27] Roche managed to actively redeploy much of its Jewish personnel to safer places, such as the United States. But the company at large remained at risk for the duration of the war. Finally, after Germany unleashed the Second World War, Roche was once again brought to the brink of bankruptcy in the 1940s because it lost access to many of its international markets due to breakdown of trade across the European continent.

If Roche and its founding family got through these crises, it was thanks in large part to the steadfast leadership of Emil Barell, who remained chairman of the board until the 1950s. During these years, Barell not only steered Roche through the turbulence; he even managed to grow the company. As far as Roche's "human capital" was concerned, there was thus no equal to the Swiss chemist.[c] (These accomplishments notwithstanding, Barell also had his shortcomings. Roche historians describe Barell as having an authoritarian bent and point out that he also made strategic and personal mistakes at times. These included misreading the major role that vitamins would go on to play in the pharma industry and falling out with one of Roche's most talented managers, Robert Boehringer, leaving the latter to reach considerable success at Geigy, a Basel competitor of Roche, instead.[28])

Roche's human capital was marked by those at the top, but also those at the base of the company. In the early years, Roche could count on many among Basel's European immigrants to join the company in its production sites. This skilled and unskilled labor force enabled Basel's industrial revolution, both in the chemical and pharmaceutical industry. They did so at a hefty price, however: many of the blue-collar workers of the city lived in shantytowns and earned only a modest wage. They nevertheless made critical contributions to Roche and other companies, without which these companies would not have been able to grow at the scale and speed they did.

Today, Basel's former working-class neighborhoods look nothing like they once did, and the low-skill, low-wage workers of that time have made way for one of the most educated and well-paid labor forces in the world. As a result, Basel is one of the most prosperous cities in the world, with the best quality of life.[d] It didn't

---

[c] Says Roche historian Alexander Bieri, "Barell's impact on Roche and its hometown of Basel was so great, in fact, that he got two honorary degrees from the University of Basel, and a street named after him in the German border town of Grenzach, where Basel's production site was based."

[d] The story between Barell and Robert Boehringer is tragic, Roche's historian Alexander Bieri says. Robert Boehringer "most probably was the only friend Barell ever had. He stemmed from the famous ultra-pietist Boehringer family, which also set up Boehringer Ingelheim and Boehringer Mannheim, but originated from the region around Stuttgart (known in German as the Piet-Cong and typically also home to a number of anthroposophical homeopathy companies). Some of Boehringer's more esoteric views—his brilliance, wit, and sharpness notwithstanding—were at odds with the Roche company culture right from the start. In the end, the two very opinionated men fell out with each other only to reconcile at Barell's death bed."

get there by sheer luck. As Roche and other industrial companies matured, so did their and the city's approach to employment. Roche heavily invested in upskilling, R&D, and university partnerships in Basel and abroad, and today counts as one of the most highly skilled workforces in the world, with about 100,000 employees spread between its Swiss headquarters (where 14,200 employees from 105 nationalities are stationed) and dozens of other locations worldwide.[29]

I don't share this story to boast about Roche, but as a reminder that human capital, too, is something you can build up over time—or that you can squander. In its first half century, my great-grandfather and Emil Barell contributed in a significant way to Roche's human capital. But if the company hadn't fostered the workforce that made their vision become reality, it would have never been able to become the powerhouse it is today. In fact, that legacy continues. Today, I believe that people come to Roche not merely to have a job, but to work together toward the company's purpose, which is "doing now what patients need next" (more about this later).

It is a lesson too for some of the most technologically advanced companies of today. I mentioned Jeff Bezos's Amazon previously. His company has brought consumers enormous benefits. Its innovations span from creating an online "everything store," to AI algorithms of same-day delivery and customized recommendation, and from Kindle e-book readers you may read this book on, to amazing Amazon Prime video content. But there is another side to this medal. Many of the people making the seamless Amazon customer experience a reality, work in warehouses or delivery services in states without labor representation or strong protections, and are stuck in low-wage jobs. Rather than to support its employees in their quest for better protections, the company has been found in at least one instance to dissuade its workers from organizing and hire anti-union consultants.[30] It would be hard to argue that this is a good way to strengthen your human capital, or create sustainable, inclusive prosperity.

Moreover, Amazon can lean on the abundant human capital of many of the world's deindustrialized cities to fuel its engine, just

as Roche could lean on the abundant human capital of the indus-
trializing Basel urban area when it first entered the scene. There
is nothing wrong with that, if it represents a transitionary phase
for business and the economy. But if people permanently remain
in low-skill, low-wage jobs, the situation is more problematic. Of
course, some developments are out of anyone's control. One reason
the Roche's workforce could upskill over time was technological
progress, and that can go either way—some technologies augment
people's work, others replace it. But valuing employees is not all
circumstantial. It is also due to the choices you make as a company.
Roche became a better employer because of the Roche union, and
its interactions with local and federal authorities that pushed for
better labor relations. When confronted with these pressures and
demands, company management and ownership made a choice:
to make good employee relations a cornerstone of Roche. Today,
more than 60% of Roche employees are members of the Roche
Employees' Association union.[31] The organization maintains regular contact with the "people and talent" department and company
management. It weighs in on salary policies, employee-friendly
working arrangements, and aims to secure Basel as an industrial
base. And it represents employees on investments committees, the
employee profit-sharing and pension committees, and the safety
and environmental protection committee.[32]

★ ★ ★

I have shared the story of Roche's "capitals" because they matter to our family company's history. Over 125 years, many more
milestone moments occurred that explain why and how Roche
became the leading pharmaceutical firm it is today. But the capitals are the foundations on which our company's success has been
built from the very beginning. They are the foundations on which
entire capitalist economies and societies are built, I would even say.

We've seen illustrations of how financial, social, natural, and
human capital are everywhere, for every company. But we've also

seen hints of how they are not always acknowledged, and sometimes even taken for granted. That is a problem, because these
capitals, like financial capital, can either grow or decline over time.
Whether they do, and to what extent, depends on the contributions we all make to them, whether we accumulate capital, or
spend them.

There is something quite special about natural, social, environmental, and human capital. They are neither entirely public nor
entirely private goods. That makes them both extremely valuable
and extremely vulnerable. They are valuable to all of us, so it is up
to each of us to leave them in a better state than we found them.
But they are vulnerable, and can be extracted, so we'll always be
tempted to consume them for our own benefit, rather than to
invest in them.

There is one final thing to know about "the capitals." They are
inseparable and interdependent. Consuming or investing in one
will influence the other. But for a long time, we pretended that
wasn't so. We believed that we could build an economy based only
on financial capital. That there could be endless growth because
there were endless resources. At times, and in certain places, we
also pretended that human and social capital were freely available,
and that they did not require investing in or contributing to. Conversely, we thought it was possible to preserve our natural capital,
even as the economy increasingly encroached on it. My father was
the embodiment of that era. Our next chapter is about him and
the people who shaped this era.

Chapter 2

A Conservationist and His Fight for the World's Natural Capital

On April 29, 1961, a group of environmentalists convened on the shores of Lake Geneva, Switzerland, and conceived of an organization we all know today: the World Wide Fund for Nature, or World Wildlife Fund (WWF), as it is also known.[1] The organization wanted to help protect endangered species around the world, such as the rhino in Eastern Africa and the panda in China. Over the decades since its founding, the WWF panda logo became an icon for every generation that grew up since, my coauthor Peter and I included.

My father, Luc Hoffmann (1923–2016), was part of this group of founders. He dedicated his life to nature conservation, serving as vice president and honorary vice president of WWF for decades. He went on to found and fund several more nature conservation organizations, too, spending a great deal of his personal wealth on the endeavor. But neither he nor the WWF could bend the arc of human development. By the time we write this book in the 2020s, a mass extinction of species has taken place, and the pressure on animal habitats continues unabated. We are still gathering funds to save the rhino and the panda, ever since the first "shock issue" supplement the WWF published in the October 9, 1961, edition of the *Daily Mirror* newspaper (see Figure 2.1).[2] A 2013 WWF campaign embodies how endangered some of these same species still are, if they haven't disappeared altogether (see Figure 2.2).

Nor are the consequences borne by animals alone. The overexploitation of nature threatens the very survival of people. At Lake Geneva, where I live, the millennia-old ecosystem centered on Alpine freshwater is at risk due to the rapidly melting Rhone valley

Figure 2.1 Snapshot of the original seven-page WWF supplement appealing for funds to save endangered species in the *Daily Mirror*, October 9, 1961.

Source: with permission of Reach PLC.

RHINO HORN IS MADE OF THE SAME STUFF AS HUMAN NAILS. STILL WANT SOME?

Figure 2.2   An ad campaign from WWF from 2013.
Source: with permission of WWF.

glaciers. In the two years ending in 2023, the nearby Mont Blanc, the highest mountain in Europe, whose name translates as the "White Mountain" for its eternally snowy top, shrunk by 2 meters due to global warming, researchers found.[3] It threatens the very source of life and wealth in one of the wealthiest regions of the world. The consequences elsewhere are an order of magnitude worse still.

How could this happen? How could it be that at a time the awareness and funding for nature is near an all-time high, there is also more destruction of natural capital than ever before in human history? How could it be that 60 years of wildlife and nature conservation efforts have come to nothing? To answer that question, allow me to take you back in time, and introduce you to my father and the world he grew up in.[a]

★ ★ ★

---

[a] I'll refer to my father always as such, and not as *Luc*, as it would be unnatural for me to do so. My apologies if this term—*my father*—therefore feels a bit overused in what follows; it is just what I always called him.

To say that my father, who passed away in 2016 at the age of 93, was passionate about nature, would be an understatement. Being in nature, and more specifically in coastal wetlands, where he could observe and study the unique birds that lived in them, was his life. I know because I lived this life. I spent most of my childhood in a house at the southern tip of the Camargue, one of the wetland regions my father was so passionate about.

We had nature in its wildest form all around us: from the mosquitoes and marshlands around our house, to the migrating flamingoes who spent their time in between the Camargue's shores and coastal West Africa. The research center my father set up to study these and other migrating birds also became our home—it was a most peculiar place to grow up in, as you might imagine! And if he wasn't watching the birds he so loved, he was attending conferences and board meetings of the WWF, the International Union for Conservation of Nature (IUCN), the MAVA Foundation for Nature, and many other organizations that shared this cause.

You may wonder, as have I, where this calling came from. Why did my father's life mission revolve around nature conservation, and not, for that matter, the fate and future of Roche, our formidable family company? The answer, as so often, is both deeply personal and profoundly circumstantial.

★ ★ ★

My father was born in Basel on January 23, 1923, at a time of global and family turmoil. The First World War had ended barely four years earlier, and the world around him lay in rubble. Imperial Germany (also known as the *Second Reich*), where most of Roche's production facilities were based—in a little town across the Rhine from Basel—had ceased to exist. The Weimar Republic that succeeded it, was marred with hyperinflation and political instability and extremism. The Russian Empire, Roche's greatest export market before the war, had given way to the communist Soviet Union, all but erasing private initiative. And most everywhere else, from France to the UK to the US, protectionism was on the rise, imperiling the international business model of the pharmaceutical multinational.

As a child, my father was shielded from many of these terrible developments, but his father, Emanuel, and especially his grandfather, Fritz, were not. Fritz had moved heaven and earth to save his company as the world around him fell apart during the 1910s. Roche had been founded at the turn of the century, as the first era of globalization reached its peak. But by the time the Great War (First World War) broke out in 1914, its foundations crumbled, and Roche went into survival mode. The war brought destruction, hyperinflation, poverty, trade restrictions, and political instability in almost every major Roche market, but especially in Europe. The company suffered enormously during those years and had to bring in external capital to survive. As a result, it did survive, albeit barely. Fritz, however, died soon after the war. He became severely ill during the tumultuous war years and died on April 18, 1920, at the age of 51.

During the years following, it fell to Fritz's son, Emanuel Hoffmann, my grandfather, to be the family's representative in the company. My grandfather was only in his 20s, and he and his wife Maja, whom he married in 1921, were also raising a growing family, which included my father (born 1923), his elder brother Andreas (born 1922), and his younger sister Vera (born 1924). In 1925, the couple and their three young children moved to Belgium, where Emanuel led Roche's Brussels office for the next five years.

After the destructive war years and their immediate aftermath (including the Spanish flu pandemic), more hopeful times followed, as Europe experienced its version of the "roaring twenties." My grandparents rode the (brief) wave of optimism with gusto. They became avid art collectors alongside their family and business duties. Their house was decorated with paintings from avant-garde painters such as Marc Chagall, Georges Braque, Pablo Picasso, and Paul Klee. Roche recovered and thrived, too, as a team of professional managers, led by Emil Barell, steered it toward new heights in Basel and around the world.

But the hopeful times my father knew as a child, weren't to last. In a quick succession of dramatic events, the world he inhabited as a child fell apart. In 1932, his father Emanuel died from the injuries he suffered in a car crash in Basel. (The family had returned to Switzerland in 1930, after their stint in Belgium.) The following year, my father's elder brother Andreas died, too, of a childhood illness. And around him, the roaring twenties made way for the terrible thirties, as unresolved political and economic issues from the First World War led to extremism. Spain and Italy fell to the authoritarian rule of Franco and Mussolini, respectively. The German Republic was captured by Adolf Hitler and the Nazi Party. As he went through his teenage years, the dark curtain that descended over Europe replaced the joyous colors of my father's childhood.

My father's response was to look for comfort in nature. He needn't go far. The "Petite Camargue" was a French nature reserve just a few kilometers upstream the Rhine from his house and the family company in Basel. It was full of creeks, marshes, and forest, and a haven for local wildlife. It was a perfect escape. He became passionate about the birds who found their refuge in the area— just like him. He started to jot down his observations, and learned everything he could about the birds. He preferred to read *Der Ornithologischer Beobachter*[4] (*The Bird Watcher*, translated to English), a Swiss scientific magazine about the fauna of the country and its surroundings, than the latest worrying geopolitical or economic news.

And so it was that when war broke out in Europe, just a few hours as the crow flies from my father's home, he found a refuge in studying birds instead. In the same year the Germans unleashed their war of expansion on the rest of Europe, at the age of 17, my father published his very first scientific article in the *Beobachter*.[5] It was the first of many contributions he would make in this field in the years and decades following, and the beginning of his lifelong devotion to nature and wildlife. He would let nothing—not the war, and not the management of Roche—get in the way of this calling.

It helped that my father was a Swiss citizen, and Switzerland was able to remain neutral in the war, despite the eerie proximity of the hostilities. (Basel, in fact, was surrounded by France and Germany, and was Switzerland's most vulnerable point for an invasion. The part of France it borders with, Alsace-Lorraine, was annexed by Germany, and had previously belong to the German Empire.) It also helped that Roche's professional management steered the company through the tumultuous war years as well as anyone could have. (To give just one example: early in the war, Emil Barell negotiated deals in France and Germany for the free passage of some of Roche's Jewish scientists to the United States. It resulted in saving some of these individuals and their families' lives, knowing what happened later in the war. But it also meant these scientists could and did continue developing drugs for Roche, which contributed to the company's postwar success.[6]) The family's involvement in Roche, meanwhile, was observed by my father's stepfather, Paul Sacher, whom his mother had married after her first husband's death.

During the war years, my father went on with his life as well as possible. He studied botany and zoology at the University of Basel, and served a mandatory period in the Swiss army, as of 1943, though he—being part of his country's neutral military—never took part in the ongoing war. As soon as his service was over, he returned to the university, and continued his study of birds as a PhD student.

After the war ended, my father took his passion for nature even further. Now in his early twenties, he felt it was time to discover the world. One day in summer 1945, he got into his car, then still a luxury, and crossed the border with France, following the decrepit but sunny roads to the Mediterranean coast. His desti-nation wasn't the "Côte d'Azur" and its beaches though—it was the Camargue and the Rhône River delta. Even more than the "Petite Camargue" where he spent his youth, the actual Camargue was home to many of Europe's most exotic bird species, and the ultimate dream of the young ornithologist. It was also an unwel-coming place. Winds and heat can make the summers unbearable for most people, as can the millions of mosquitos that inhabit its marshlands. The local population dealt with this environment well, mostly devoting themselves to raising bulls and horses, or growing rice on the endless flatlands between the river and the sea. (They also occasionally enjoyed the local pastis after a hard day's work, and right they were!) But my father fell in love with this land and its people, including dozens of birds found nearly nowhere else in Europe. He decided to make this hostile, forgotten land his home. In 1947, he bought an old but stately Mediterranean farm house (locally known as *mas*) in the heart of the natural reserve and settled there. He was later joined there by my mother Daria, whom he married in 1954.

From that time on, the paths of my father, the sole male heir of the Hoffmann family, and Roche, which was once again recovering and expanding under its professional leadership, diverged.[b] Under the vice-chairmanship of my step-grandfather, the family's rule was to not get involved with Roche too closely. The family, under Sacher's guidance, would supervise professional management from the board, and try and restore the family's majority voting rights, which had been lost in the interbellum. But it would no longer manage the company day by day. For Sacher, it allowed time to focus on his professional passion, which was music. He was an orchestra conductor and a patron of the arts. But the approach also served my father well. For almost half a century, he did serve on the Roche board, but he always kept at arm's length. He would rather spend his time on his passion, in the Camargue and elsewhere.

It was in this family setting that I grew up, born in 1958. I was the only boy of four siblings: Vera (born 1954), Maja (born 1956), and Daria (born 1960–†2019). As my father built an ornithological station next to our house—or more accurately, as he made a family home next to his ornithological station!—we were homeschooled.

---

[b] I should stress that the divergence was not due to the presence of my mother Daria. She supported my father in the choices he made, personally and professionally, but never interfered in the relationship between him and the company.

We went to school in a purpose-built classroom next door to our *mas*, together with the sons and daughters of my father's fellow researchers and other locals. We could see firsthand how impactful the growing influence of my father on nature conservation was, at home and abroad. At home, he was instrumental in helping protect the Camargue as a French natural reserve. My father became the biggest private landowner in the region, protecting thousands more acres from development. As he invited fellow conservationists and researchers to our home and the research station, he also expanded his own conservation efforts. And we often accompanied him on his travels around the world, too, seeing with our own eyes both how badly the protection of wildlife was, and what difference my father's efforts made, whether in the Mediterranean or further south, on the African continent.

My father played a key role, for example, in protecting the immense Doñana National Park in Southern Spain from the 1960s onwards. This park is considered the most biodiverse natural space of Europe, and hosts dozens of rare species of birds, mammals, reptiles, and amphibians including the imperial eagle, the black stork, the mora turtle, and the Iberian lynx, one of the most threatened animals on the planet.[7] If it wasn't for the efforts of my father and his fellow conservationists, it may have been lost to agricultural and tourist development. In the years following, my father helped identify many more such parks and wetlands in need of preservation, as vice president of the International Union for the Conservation of Nature. His WWF cofounding was in that regard both a crowning achievement, and the start of the institution's global, multidecade journey, with a legacy that continues to the present day. My father remained the WWF's vice president until 1988. During that time, the WWF scored some major wins in preventing the extinction of some of the most at-risk species. And if all that wasn't enough, my father created the MAVA foundation in the early 1990s. He set up the organization to support biodiversity projects and promote a more sustainable economy. Over the course of the organization's 25-year lifespan, our family provided MAVA with some

1 billion Swiss francs (about $1.15 billion), coming from dividends of Roche shares we owned.

★ ★ ★

But for all these successes, a bigger picture has emerged in recent decades, and it hasn't been a pretty one. In truth, philanthropists have failed to recognize the complexity of the environmental challenge (or have at least failed in addressing them effectively and on a global scale). Since the WWF was founded, nature has suffered more setbacks than wins. More species are disappearing every year. And the planet's ability to replenish itself and provide for either human or animal needs is diminishing. We need a different model to protect and benefit from nature.

This is not to suggest my father' generation did not do valuable work—on the contrary. Without them, the state of nature would be much worse still. The ideals they had were laudable, the individual contributions they made to conservation were almost superhuman. And who am I to judge the way society at large, and individuals such as my father specifically, dealt with the conflicts, traumas, and setbacks they lived through during the 1930s and 1940s? If nothing else, the economic model our parents' and grandparents' generations devised after the war prevented another world war and led to widely held human prosperity and development. All the while, my father and his peers made sure the broader impact on nature and animal life wasn't forgotten.

But we do know now that the economic system they were part of was flawed and out of balance. In fact, in his later years, my father saw that with his own eyes. On a global scale, of course, global warming and climate change have reached untenable heights. It is due to the industrial model of the 20th century, and its reliance on cheap but harmful fossil fuels and the exploitation and destruction of nature. It is also true on a personal level. All the philanthropy my father engaged in could not weigh up against the environmental damage caused by all kinds of companies—including ours—and the industries they were part of.

During the boom years after the war particularly, economic development outweighed almost any other concern. The destruction of nature and biodiversity was and still is the other side of the same coin. If conservation efforts failed, it was mostly because there was a division between idealistic "tree huggers" on the one hand and amoral businesses on the other. (I use *amoral* here in the sense that businesses followed the logic of the "invisible hand," absolving them of the requirement to actively seek to make moral decisions, and think through their nonfinancial consequences.) What should have happened instead—and what needs to happen still—was for business to integrate a nature and biodiversity agenda. I often say that to have an impact, "it is not how you spend money, but how you make it." Nothing good was ever going to come from allowing business to pursue profits and ignore its externalities on the one hand, and then hope that individual philanthropic efforts were going to make up for it on the other.

It is a reality that both my father and I became aware of. At what moment in his career this happened to my father, I cannot say, though he and I discussed it several times toward the end of his life. But my penny dropped when I was faced with an ethical dilemma as vice-chairman of Roche a couple of years ago, which I'll describe next. As of the 1920s, Roche started to use chemical synthesis in the production of some of its products, including vitamins. By the turn of the 21st century, that legacy came to haunt us.

★ ★ ★

By its very nature, producing pharmaceutical products often relies on chemical processes, whether extraction or synthesis based. Pragmatically, Roche also expanded into the production of chemicals, given the Rhine region's prowess in the industry, and made several acquisitions in the chemical industry. In the 1960s, for example, Roche acquired Geneva-based Givaudan, a fragrances and flavors maker. Givaudan relied heavily on synthetical chemical processes to create its main products, and also had a small unit producing disinfectants.

Chemistry and chemical processes can be wonderful when they go as intended, but they can also cause a lot of harm when they go wrong. Our family company found that out firsthand. In July 1976, an accident occurred in a Givaudan-owned chemical plant in Seveso, Italy. When shutting down the plant operations for the weekend, a batch process was stopped before its completion, which subsequently caused a vessel in the factory to overheat. The resulting pressure was given off to the environment by a safety valve. Due to the overheating of the vessel, dioxin had formed unintentionally.[8] That proved disastrous for the natural environment and its inhabitants. Several thousands of small farm animals died or were killed to prevent further spread of the dioxin to humans. Hundreds of local inhabitants suffered from skin injuries, and—following medical advice because of perceived risks—more than two dozen women opted for an abortion of their pregnancy. The disaster was later qualified as one of the worst environmental disasters in history by *TIME Magazine*.[9] In any case, it took years before Roche, the parent company, could confirm that all the harmful dioxin was permanently removed. Several Givaudan executives in Italy were condemned in court.

Other impacts happened closer to home and involved Roche more directly still. As Roche expanded in the postwar decades in Europe, marked by rapid economic growth, so did its chemical and environmental footprint. Chemical production also meant chemical waste. Lacking any standards on disposal, Roche and several other chemical companies in the Basel area agreed with authorities to dump their chemical waste in a pit along the Rhine, the Kesslergrube. The practice went on for several decades. No one knew any better, including the authorities, and when the pit was finally full, it was literally covered up. As time went by, this legacy was almost forgotten. Different approaches for these chemical processes emerged, and ultimately, Roche stopped producing such large quantities of harmful chemical waste altogether. It divested some activities, improved others, and discontinued yet others. But the enormous amounts of chemical waste produced during the postwar economic boom years remained in the pit along the Rhine. If it ever leaked into the Rhine, it could cause another public health disaster.

Almost half a century later, the file was reopened. I had joined the board of Roche in the mid-1990s, and by 2006, had become vice-chairman. A few years later, in 2014, the local authorities in Germany decided it was time to take another look at the Kesslergrube. It decided that the companies that were historically responsible for the waste had to do something about it. To me, it was clear what we should do: clean up our act. We put some of our best safety, health, and environment engineers on the job, and they came up with a clean but costly solution. Most importantly, new incineration solutions had come to the market, and we could put them to use in the Kesslergrube. By burning the waste at extremely high temperatures in a specially made incinerator, we could turn the toxic material into harmless ashes. What was more, whatever waste could not be incinerated, could be transported safely over the Rhine to the Netherlands, and treated there. In all, the risk of contamination could be reduced to zero, and the environmental impact brought back to a minimum. But there was a downside: it would cost the company hundreds of millions of euros, without any short-term financial return. (The long-term pay-off, of course, would be that any future environmental disaster and Roche's liability for it would be averted, leading to a reduced risk profile of the site.) Together with our board and management, we decided the investment was worth it. In a sustainable, responsible form of capitalism, the polluter pays for the negative externalities they cause. We wanted to lead by example.

★ ★ ★

The logic of the rule that the "polluter pays" has been missing in the 20th-century economic system. (Except, that is, in some economic theories, such as that of Arthur Pigou, who argued starting the 1920s for a "Pigouvian tax" on externalities caused by companies[10]—to not much avail until recently.) By compartmentalizing the roles of business, government, and civil society in lanes that are too narrow, moreover, a lot of externalities haven't even been accounted for at all. It is an original sin of postwar capitalism. To overcome this design error, no philanthropy or NGO effort could ever be enough. What we need is a sustainable, inclusive form of capitalism, with new principles, and new practices. In such a system, the business of business isn't just business. The business of business is to at least preserve and where possible expand the world's human, social, environmental, and financial capital.

In such a world, disasters such as the one in the Givaudan factory in Seveso would be less likely to occur, and if they did, a company wouldn't argue for years over its responsibility or the need to make right what it had done wrong. A company also wouldn't produce toxic waste to begin with, as happened in the Kesslergrube site near Roche's headquarters along the Rhine. If it did, it would include the cost for remediating this harm into its business model. Nor would any responsible company suggest privatizing and potentially destroying one of the world's most valuable ecosystems. That is what happened in the Doñana National Park, until my father and fellow WWF founders intervened and bought parts of the park with their personal funds. Nor would farmers or agribusinesses drain valuable marshlands any further to make way for intensive agriculture, which is what happened in the Camargue for decades into the 20th century. In such a world, the role of business—like that of other stakeholders—would be very different. It is this new world and this model of capitalism that I strive for.

★ ★ ★

Why didn't we get there before? A big part of the explanation is that at some point, we started to believe that there was no need to think about what is "right" and "wrong" in terms of business actions. The market would figure that out all on its own, with Adam Smith's invisible hand ensuring that all would be well in economy and society. All we had to calculate was which business practice was most profitable. This was magical thinking. There is a straight line between economist Milton Friedman's statement in 1970, that "the social responsibility of business is to increase its profits," and the laissez-faire capitalism that prevailed in the West for much of the past 50 years, which led to the unsustainable and highly unequal global economy we have today.

But I do understand why the likes of Friedman endorsed these rallying cries. I understand also why a writer like Ayn Rand, who was "radical for capitalism," advocated freedom above all else. These individuals feared that communism or another form of totalitarianism would prevail if economic freedom and the pursuit of profit weren't radically protected. To them, *that* was the worst-case scenario we had to prevent at all costs. They weren't wrong in worrying over how poorly the world would fare if communism replaced capitalism. My mother and her family fell victim to this dystopian reality. From the late 1930s onwards, life, liberty, and property rights as they knew them ended in the lands they came from—Austria and Czechoslovakia. It cost them nearly all their possessions, and society as they knew it never recovered.

★ ★ ★

While my father was studying back in neutral Switzerland, my mother, Daria Razumovsky (1925–2002), was experiencing the war and its destruction in a more direct way. She came from an aristocratic family that gained wealth and notoriety in the Austro-Hungarian Empire. She lived with her sisters and parents between Vienna and their estate in Czechoslovakia. The First World War, which ended seven years before my mother was born, dealt a cataclysmic blow to the Razumovskys' world. The once mighty Austrian empire gave way to a disparate collection of much smaller nation-states. But it was the Second World War and its aftermath, which my mother lived through as a young adult, that destroyed their world for good. As the Nazis annexed Austria and captured Sudetenland in the late 1930s, my mother and her sisters realized their life would never be the same, they wrote in their diary.[11] In the years following, the entirety of their homeland was occupied, and the family was dispossessed from their estate. They never recuperated it. When the rest of Europe was liberated, Czechoslovakia soon got trapped behind the "Iron Curtain." In the communist regime that followed, private property was abolished altogether. The Razumovskys retreated to Austria, their titles, possessions, and social network lost in the chaos of the turmoil of the 20th century.

In the grand scheme of things, a reader might argue that it matters little that a well-off family suffered material losses during and after the war. I understand that. But my point is that no one else in Czechoslovakian society gained from it. The outcome of the communists' power grab wasn't more prosperity for everyone else. It was less prosperity for everyone, and an absolute loss of freedom and rights for society at large. It was this threat, which still lingered in the 1960s and 1970s, that radicalized economic thinkers such as Friedman and Rand. They had seen what happened when economic and individual freedoms were curtailed in the name of misplaced righteousness. Communism was full of "good" ethics and principles, such as the slogan "from each according to his ability, to each according to his needs." But it ended up in poverty, corruption, and misuse of power.

The best way to prevent these communist principles from gaining a foothold in the US and Western Europe, free-market capitalists believed, was to insist on radical economic freedom, free of moral principles. They were convinced that was a much better basis to build economic and social life on, and that it would lead to much greater prosperity. When the communist bloc collapsed at the end of the 1980s, they were vindicated. But 35 years on, we know their vindication was only a snapshot in a longer history. Compared with Soviet communism, laissez-faire capitalism was indeed by far the better choice. But by taking freedoms to the extreme, and ownership over externalities to a bare minimum, the free-market capitalism Friedman and others exhorted created a whole new set of problems.

★ ★ ★

For all the good they did, the generation of my father did initially go along with one of Friedman's underlying beliefs: that everyone was best off staying in their own lane. Conservationists tried to save the environment not by changing business, but by delineating up to where it could go. Wetlands, wildlife reserves and endangered species were off-limits. But by merely debating where their lane ended and the one from business started, they won a Pyrrhic victory. Business, meanwhile, expanded its global footprint, without questioning its broader impact. It propelled humanity forward, but also created all kinds of harmful externalities to the environment and societies en passant. There was no resolution of the underlying conflict, because there was no alternative model—other than communism. The result is the imbalance among the world's capitals—human, social, environmental, and financial—we know today.

If we want to get out of this Catch 22, we need to change the concept of everyone being better off by staying in their own lanes. The better mental image is this one: we are all swimming in the same pool, using the same water to get ahead. If someone muddies the water in their lane, or creates a tidal wave, it is going to spill over to the rest of the pool. They may benefit from this kind of behavior in the short run, but what goes around, comes around. If we want to keep enjoying our common pool, we'll all have to accept a shared responsibility over the water that keeps us all afloat.

If we apply that image back to conservationism, prosperity, and business, it means business should think not just about how it can create a profit but also how it can do so in a way that benefits society and the environment. If activities create negative environmental externalities, such as waste, pollution, or the destruction of animal or human habitats, business should offset those, or, if that is not possible, incur any associated cost. The better approach is for business to focus on finding "nature-based solutions," which enable nature to sustain itself over time or better yet, regenerate itself. The same principle should apply to the creation or destruction of human and social capital. The goal of business should be to increase the capitals, not to maximize one of them—financial capital—at the expense of reducing the others. Such a model would prevent much conflict among societal actors to begin with because there are shared objectives, and an incorporation of costs for causing harm. It would also make philanthropy both less needed and more effective, as business would be better at answering society's needs than it is today.

Despite recent progress, however, we are far from that ideal. That is because a more short-term, neoliberal version of capitalism is still dominant in our world today, and its impact runs from business school to board rooms. It is that legacy that we will dive into in Chapter 3.

Chapter 3

Finding the Compass for a New Nature of Business

In some ways, Roche was doing very well when I joined its board in 1996, a hundred years after its founding. It was just about the largest pharmaceutical company in the world, with a portfolio consisting of some of the most innovative and most essential medicines. Each year, it helped millions of patients. It provided tens of thousands of jobs and returned its shareholders with handsome dividends. Yet there were growing areas of concern, too. The company was losing market share in its most profitable markets, and losing sight of its purpose, investing in a variety of non-core activities.

Even so, it shocked me to learn that US prosecutors alleged Roche was also doing something else: leading a price-fixing ring. Roche had for years colluded with its competitors, the prosecutor said, to keep

---

This chapter is written in André's voice.

the price of certain vitamins in the US market artificially high. That had enabled it and other participating companies to share in the profits and had cheated US consumers from billions of dollars. It was quite an accusation, and quite a welcome for me as the new face of the family shareholders. The court also considered the accusation proven. As a result, Roche was handed almost a billion dollars in fines, by courts in both the US and—a few years later—Europe.

To make matters worse, at around the same time Roche also had to withdraw two drugs it had recently launched on the market, at great expense. The company had belatedly discovered adverse side effects, which made them a hazard for certain patients. The only right thing left to do was to pull the drugs from the market, despite their proven efficacy, and despite hundreds of millions of lost R&D, marketing, and sales costs. The two cases hurt the company's bottom line. But they were also a signal that our company's governance was failing. Before I could propose any high-minded agenda, our company had to straighten itself up.

★ ★ ★

Business, I believe, should create sustainable and inclusive prosperity. But for decades, the entire Western business community was mesmerized by another logic: that of the power of free markets, and most of all, by a belief in an all-encompassing "invisible hand." To introduce a new paradigm, I had to first learn, then unlearn, everything about how business works.

Growing up in the shielded environment of the Camargue and a Swiss private school, I was at first ignorant about the role of business in society as a child and adolescent. My family's ties to the company it founded had been largely reduced to picking up a check every year in Basel when profits were distributed. I didn't even know the difference between a share and a bond, let alone that I had any idea about Roche's core activities in research and development (R&D).

As for Roche, through the postwar years, it had always kept a focus on helping patients. But during a few decades before my arrival, it was doing much more than that, too. At some point, it wasn't even clear anymore from its financial statements what its core business really was. How could we turn that around? And how could I play a leading role in this turnaround? These were the challenges I progressively encountered as I took on a more prominent role in the company. They were the challenges of capitalism at large, too, I would say, so our learnings may be helpful for others as well.

★ ★ ★

As I came of age in the late 1970s and early 1980s, I learned a lot about the wider world. Until I started high school in Switzerland, I had led an almost fairytale-like life in the Camargue. I could tell you which birds migrated when in the Mediterranean, but I didn't know the first thing about doing business. My step-grandfather, Paul Sacher, had always kept a significant distance between the family and Roche, and my father had taken that a step further. He was out to save the world through nature conservation efforts, not by getting involved in a pharmaceutical business. But that hands-off approach also had some unintended consequences. Over time, it became clear to me that my family was seen as *Glückspilze* by management. (Literally, this German expression means "lucky mushrooms" in English, but perhaps "lucky devils" is a better translation.) The company's leadership saw us as not so business-savvy—a group of people who were fortunate to have a controlling interest in Roche. With that attitude toward us, however, professional management was also less likely to take our oversight seriously. Neither side of that equation was a recipe for success, I realized later.

For the time being, I was looking for my own way in life. And as I did, it started to dawn on me that I needed to educate myself about business. "Are you from *the* Hoffmann family, from

Hoffmann-La Roche," a fellow college student once asked me in those years, baffled that I seemed to know little if anything about the company. "Yes," I acknowledged hesitantly. And so, for most of the 1980s and early 1990s, after initially studying medicine, I immersed myself instead in the world of mainstream economics, finance, and business. I studied economics at the Swiss university of St. Gallen; worked a few years in the City, London's financial center; and capped my formal training with an MBA from INSEAD, the French business school, and a stint at Nestlé, the Swiss multinational company.

If I could be considered a *Glückspilz* at the end of the 1970s, unaware of even the most basic business principles, by the mid-1990s I was well versed in mainstream business and management knowledge. The time was ripe to make a more active contribution to Roche. I got the trust of the family "pool" of shareholders to replace my father and step-grandfather as family representative on the board. (At the same time, my cousin Andreas was elected by his branch of the family to replace his father on the board.) But, as I quickly learned, we had our work cut out for us, and my background in business and finance was as much a handicap as it was a help. The mainstream management theories and economic principles of the time turned out to be poor pillars to build a 21st-century company on.

The view of the world put forth by Milton Friedman and other Chicago School economists, which I had learned about in school, and which was practiced in London's City, was really one of amorality and purposelessness. "There is one and only one social responsibility of business," Friedman wrote in a 1970 *New York Times* essay, describing his doctrine.[1] "That responsibility is . . . to make as much money as possible." (The only caveat he put was that shareholders have the last say—but he immediately added that they generally prefer for the company to make money—and that companies must "conform to the basic rules of society.") It wasn't up to company management to "contribute to the social objective of preventing inflation . . . or . . . of improving the environment . . . or . . . of reducing poverty," Friedman believed. Following the "shareholder primacy" point of view, such practices "would be spending someone else's money for a general social interest."

I saw this logic at work as it gained popularity in Margaret Thatcher's United Kingdom of the 1980s, which coincided with when it became dominant in Ronald Reagan's America as well. At first, there seemed no reason to question this doctrine—to the contrary. From my desk in the City, I witnessed an economy on fire. From 1982 onwards, the stock and bond markets went on a five-year winning spree. More mergers and acquisitions (M&A) took place every day. The market in bonds and other financial products was booming, turning many traders and investors on Wall Street and the City into (multi-)millionaires almost overnight. Despite a financial crisis in Asia later in the 1980s, it seemed Friedmanite economics would create prosperity forever. After I returned from business school in 1990, post–Iron Curtain euphoria heralded another decade of globalization and stock market bull runs. It was easy to get dazzled by this seemingly never-ending good news show. But below the surface, problems started to brew.

The first problem was that if companies didn't know what they stood for, or what they were meant to do, they had no compass to follow, other than making money. In the US, companies like General Electric and Enron were the epitome of this logic. General Electric had long been an American industrial pioneer. Founded by Thomas Edison, the company helped electrify the US in the early 1900s. It started a new era of industrialization and set the country up for its global economic dominance. But by the 1980s, it was hard to say what GE was anymore, beyond a financial conglomerate.[a] Its nonstop buying and selling of companies earned it a top spot in the Fortune 500 list, as one of America's

---

[a] An excellent source for the story of GE and its link to the Friedman doctrine is David Gelles's 2023 book *The Man Who Broke Capitalism*.

largest companies by revenues. But it also turned it into a giant with feet of clay. GE's 1986 purchase of Kidder, Peabody & Co, a major financial securities firm, should have been a warning sign. A mere eight years later it was sold at a major loss. But oddly GE's halo lasted for another decade or two, until it finally started a rapid descent in revenues, earnings, and stock price starting in the 2000s. (Today, GE is split up into three entities, much smaller than the 1980s conglomerate, but each with a much clearer purpose.)

Enron was an even worse cautionary tale—it descended into *immorality*. The Texas-based firm started as an energy company, but by the end of the 1990s, no one really knew anymore what Enron did, except that it looked like financial wizardry. The company filed for bankruptcy in 2001. It had been nothing more than a financial house of cards, it turned out.

The second problem was that this kind of casino capitalism was starting to have harmful, real-world consequences for the economy and society at large. The received wisdom about capitalism—coming almost directly from Milton Friedman—was that you needn't worry about the social, economic, or environmental consequences of your actions, as long as they were not illegal. But in a system in which short-term financial gains ruled over all other considerations, long-term problems started to surface, such as rising market concentration and prices, increased income inequality, and a faltering appreciation for R&D, not to mention the environmental problems discussed previously in this book.

One reason for this situation was a seemingly inconspicuous change at the top of corporations. By the early 1980s, shareholders had started to believe they faced a "principal-agent problem," following a theory developed by US economists Michael Jensen and William Meckling.[2] It held that conflicts of interest would inevitably emerge between shareholders of a company and professional management because their intrinsic interests did not align. Shareholders, in this theory, would simply want the maximum financial return on their investment. Professional managers, not being owners, might want to spend corporate money on all kinds of other purposes, including self-enrichment, corporate handouts, or other frivolous expenses. That was the theory. To solve that possible misalignment, corporate remuneration started to include stocks and stock options as executive compensation. It was meant to ensure that both the principal (the stockholder) and the agent (professional management) had the same (financial) interests.

Over time, though, the system backfired. Short-term financial considerations became even more important in the minds of managers, while their executive compensation skyrocketed to never-seen-before heights. In the management of a firm, nonfinancial considerations largely disappeared into the background. A couple of macro-economic statistics reveal just how profound the combined effects of the principal-agent theory and the free-market ideology of Milton Friedman were. In the US, CEO pay went up more than 1,200% in the past five decades, driven in great part by variable compensation in the form of stocks and stock options. The average worker's salary, meanwhile, increased by only about 15% in the US,[3] and the labor share of GDP fell in almost every major economy.[4] As financial incentives became more prominent, both for executives and stockholders, especially during the 1980s and 1990s, M&A activities soared. Logically, market concentration rose in almost every sector of the economy, and markups in those industries also went up. R&D, meanwhile, underwent a major transformation too, and not a good one. Governments started to spend less on R&D, leaving those kinds of investments to the private sector. And even though R&D spent among business did indeed go up in the 1980s and beyond, the appreciation of the stock market for them went down.[5] The scientific community at large, meanwhile, started to come up with fewer and fewer disruptive innovations.[6]

Seen from a shareholder perspective, you might wonder what the problem was with these macro-economic trends, if they solved the principal-agent problem and focused business on their core job: making money for shareholders. Who really cares if economic inequality rises among the working population, or if executives get better compensation, if it means shareholders get a better return on their investment? Why would you worry about increasing market concentration and price markups if you're an owner of one of the resulting superstar firms? If anything, conventional thinking should lead you to applaud such developments. At first, like pretty much everyone else I knew in the City, on Wall Street, in management circles, or the boardroom, I did not immediately question the financial levers propelling the economy forward from the 1980s onwards. But when a corporate raider entered the capital of Roche in the 1990s; Roche got almost a billion dollars in fines for price-fixing in the US and Europe[7] in 1999 and 2001; and we got a call about the family shares in the early 2000s, it became progressively clear to me something was *very* wrong with the underpinnings of this system and its reverberations on corporate management.

★ ★ ★

There were few immovable principles in my family's long ownership of Roche. One perspective, however, never changed: that what is good for the company, is good for the family, and not the other way around. Conversely, we believed it was good for Roche—and for society—that the company had a long-term oriented owner. As a family, we were naturally inclined to take a multigenerational outlook on business. We had also been rooted in Basel and Switzerland since long before the creation of our family business and were aware how much this society had enabled us to prosper. We wanted to help sustain and build the prosperity of our city and society, too. That was a self-interested perspective, of course, but also one that was clearly more enlightened than that of an investor obsessed with short-term returns. If we wanted this mutually beneficial relationship with the company, society, and the family to continue, we should stay invested in the company and maintain a majority of the voting stock.

During our more than 100-year history, we had come close to giving up our ownership once before. It served as a warning for the family ever since. In the 1930s, Alfred Hoffmann, the brother of my grandfather, Emmanuel, and fellow heir to the family company, decided he wanted out. When Alfred sold his half of shares to a local consortium controlled by Emil Barell, and my grandfather Emmanuel died prematurely, the family majority voting rights hung in the balance. It was then that my step-grandfather Paul Sacher (my grandmother's second husband), took charge, and restored the family's position in the company. He acted as custodian of the shares my grandmother had inherited and made a successful bid to buy back Alfred's shares. He was happy to delegate day-to-day management to professional management because he felt the company had capable leaders within its ranks.

But to let go of ownership also meant to imperil the prosperous ties between the family and the city. He warned future generations, including myself, not to let that happen. In 1996, as he stepped down from the Roche board at age 90, it was from him that I took over the board seat. It was my turn to oversee the relationship with Roche, the family, and society. But the honeymoon period didn't last very long. Instead, the next few years were like an extended baptism of fire and sneak peek into what had gone wrong with capitalism.

★ ★ ★

The first cataclysmic event to hit our company was the price-fixing scandal. (As a reminder: it all started when a US prosecutor had brought a case against Roche and others, claiming the companies had for years colluded with each other to keep the price of certain vitamins in the market artificially high and pump up their profits.) Roche's defense at the time was that the situation wasn't as black and white as the US and European prosecutors had claimed, and that the market had been fundamentally distorted by dumping, which explained the need for other suppliers to maintain a higher price. But in the greater scheme of things, it missed a more important consideration: Roche had no strategic reason anymore to be in the vitamin business. Vitamins had been a meaningful and worthwhile part of our business until the 1950s and 1960s, providing health benefits to many people around the world. But by the 1990s, the company had built up an impressive track record in innovative drug development and made that—lifesaving, specialty treatments—a core pursuit of the company. It was where its strengths now lay; it was what its corporate DNA was all about. Vitamins had become a commodity, far removed from the unique, innovative drugs Roche was known for. Was there still a point to offering them and being a conglomerate company?

The second wake-up call was the withdrawal of a new drug from the US market in 1998, Posicor, because of observed adverse side effects with some patients.[8] To this day, for an R&D-oriented company like Roche, launching new patented drugs that patients need is at the very core of what we are about. It determines our usefulness to society, and it is crucial in maintaining a profitable business model over time. When we fumbled on the launch of these new drugs, by not fully realizing their side effects, all of a sudden it didn't matter anymore that other parts of the company were making huge profits. What mattered was that we were failing in our core assignment, which was to make patients better. If we couldn't guarantee that our products helped people, what was really left of our reason for being?

The third and final challenge, for the company and more directly for our family's ownership, was the threat of a takeover. That threat had first appeared when an activist investor started to amass voting shares in Roche in the 1990s. It came to a head when those shares were sold to Roche's Basel neighbor Novartis, and we received a call about the remaining family shares. Among the family members, our immediate gut reaction was to oppose any possible sale. But we were forced to explain to ourselves, as well as to Roche management, employees, and shareholders, why that was the case, and why Roche was better off as an independent unit. What was the point of remaining a stand-alone company?

At first sight, those three issues may seem to have little in common, and you may wonder what they have to do with the developments in management and economic theory I described previously. But in essence, they all came down to the same question: what is the purpose of our company? And that question was one almost all companies in the US and Europe were ultimately confronted with, sooner or later.

In our case, somewhere in the mid-1980s, Roche management— like the management of many companies at the time—started leaning heavily on financial profits as a measure of success. The circumstances Roche faced were unique to the company, but the broader context in which the shift took place was similar for everyone. In 1985, the patent on Roche's most valuable drug, Valium, had come to an end, and that forced management to figure out what to do next. For more than two decades, Valium had been one of the best-selling drugs in the world. In the US it was even the most-sold drug of any company for 15 years, selling more than 2 billion doses a year at its peak.[9] In this way, Valium had become vital to Roche's financial success. So, when the patent ended, management started looking for other ways to maintain its growth and profitability. Orthodox management thinking, as I explained, was to seek financial growth and profitability wherever it was available. Roche management still invested in new R&D. But it also did what everyone else was doing: buy other companies and make financial investments.

When I looked at the kind of company Roche had become after more than a decade of pursuing this approach, I found a sprawling enterprise. Sure enough, we had promising new drugs in development because we had never stopped investing in research. We had also made some excellent acquisitions of companies that like Roche were at the cutting edge of science. But there were also odd elements in our balance sheet. Givaudan, the fragrance maker, was still on the books. We still made vitamins, despite this not being our core business anymore. And overall, it turned out that a small financial department of a handful of people was making nearly as much money as the entire rest of the company. That was great as long as it lasted. But it also meant that investments going wrong could bring the entire company in danger. And as the vitamins case had shown, noncore assets could distract management, cause financial headaches, or even cost us the trust of authorities and society at large. This was not a solid foundation to build the Roche of the future on.

But selling to Novartis wouldn't be the right answer, either. It would continue the Friedmanite form of capitalism and turn "NovaRoche" into a local monopoly. For the family, there would be the prospect of a major payout, of course, running in the dozens of billions of dollars. But what of other stakeholders? If anything, the move would further concentrate power in the industry, without a clear advantage to patients. The combined company would most likely be driven by short-term financial objectives. A rationalization of the workforce was almost certain to occur, and a cost-cutting drive in R&D would be next. The city of Basel was likely to lose out, too. Our belief, as later expressed by our CEO, was that it was better to have strong competition. M&A have a useful purpose in capitalism, and we have kept on pursuing them in recent years. But if the overarching logic behind them is short-term or monopoly gains, rather than a long-term strategic fit, they are bound to create more harm than good.

★ ★ ★

In the early years on the company board, I didn't yet see things as clearly as I see them now. Our journey as the next generation of owners started in a small town in central Switzerland called Feldmeilen in the early 2000s. The immediate question that lay in front of us at the time was whether we wanted the family to retain control of Roche, and if so, in what form. I knew which answer I favored, but it was nevertheless an uphill battle, and one that would immediately be followed by a whole new set of challenges.

Not only would we have to face off with Novartis interest and wavering public support but also Roche's then top management also questioned how capable we were as owners. Within the family, moreover, the longest-standing ties with the company had disappeared within a few short years, as my father and (step-)grandfather had retired a few years earlier, at the company's 100-year anniversary in 1996. We were being squeezed from all sides.

To turn the tide, I put forward to the family an agenda for Roche based on three pillars: unity as owners, a new relationship with management, and a focus on purpose and profitability.[b] They all had a distinctive reason, and different role to play.

Unity as Owners

The best owner for any company, I believe, is one that is stable, long-term oriented, and deeply committed to the success of the company and its stakeholders. Across the corporate spectrum, such owners mostly belong to either of the following three groups: local governments, foundations, and founding families. We obviously fall into the last category and fit most criteria. But by the early 2000s, we no longer had a deep, shared commitment to the company we owned. We needed to reverse that trend.

One strength we could build on was that we never lost our ties to Basel. My side of the family had moved to the Camargue, and later to the French-speaking part of Switzerland around Lake Geneva. But as a family, we remained invested in the prosperity of our town of origin. The family of my aunt Vera had remained in Basel, for example, and become patrons of culture, science, education, and arts.

---

[b] I had to gain the trust of my family as their representative, help the company regain the trust of society, and give Roche a north star toward purpose and profitability. It took time, but we succeeded in that journey, and the improvements helped Roche end up in a much better place. More broadly, I hope they can also symbolize a different approach to the role business can play in society.

During our family meetings in Feldmeilen, we agreed on a joint commitment to the company, and that we would "show" ourselves once again as owners: First, we renewed our unity as family shareholders, giving the company the stability and long-term outlook that was expected from us. We would also meet at regular intervals, and discuss key matters related to the company and the family. And second, we decided to communicate to the outside world that we would be active, hands-on family owners again, concerned with the long-term success of the company and its home base. As part of that, we wanted to make sure the enthusiasm and commitment we felt again flowed over onto employees and other stakeholders. We wanted to inspire Roche and exude confidence.

New Relationship with Management

The key place for us to interact with management was and remained the boardroom. My cousin Andreas and I replaced my father, my step-grandfather, and my uncle as family board members. But we wanted to make sure the board was not a place to simply rubberstamp management plans. The board needed to engage in the actual governance and oversight of the company.

One important element in this regard was the creation of board committees, including the remuneration committee, the corporate governance and sustainability committee, and the audit committee. The first was created to streamline CEO and management pay, which until recently had been the result of a cigar-and-cognac meeting between the CEO and my step-grandfather, Paul Sacher. The second was created to convey that as owners, we were serious about the long-term viability of our company, and that good governance and environmental stewardship were part of that. The third one, finally, resulted from a new legal requirement.

The professionalization of the board sent a signal to top management. In the 1980s and 1990s, while the new business paradigm of "shareholder primacy" took hold across the corporate world, another reality emerged in our company. It was one where the family owners, led by Paul Sacher, were largely uninvolved in day-to-day management, and management lost interest in maintaining a business relationship with the family.[c] The creation of board committees changed that dynamic. It indicated we were serious about the key levers of corporate performance and culture, and about the oversight we intended to keep over the company identity. It also reminded top management that they served a greater purpose.

Focus on Purpose and Profitability

By the time we met in Feldmeilen, we had become aware that Roche was vulnerable, and was not living up to its full potential. I came to believe that underlying that long-term financial underperformance was a company that was no longer solely driven by purpose. We had received warning signs before. Our failed product launches and the fine for price-fixing were a reminder of the risk we took by taking our eyes off the ball. They were moves driven by the lure of short-term profits but ended costing us dearly in the long run. It was for this reason that financial investments in noncore assets, though profitable for now, were a bad idea, too.

Roche's new management went to work with this new strategic imperative. Roche divested most of its noncore assets, including the Givaudan fragrances business and the vitamin business. Those decisions worked out for all parties involved: Givaudan became sustainable as an independent company, and DSM, the buyer of our vitamins division, successfully integrated that business in its own transformation plans.

---

[c] There was, however, always a great amount of mutual respect. Roche's senior management, for example, admired Paul Sacher and my father for what they were doing in the world of music and the environment, and vice versa, but each side also understood it was not their cup of tea, so to speak.

(One example illustrates well why selling these noncore businesses made sense for Roche from a "purpose" perspective. One of the vitamins Roche made for decades was astaxanthin. It is a precursor of Vitamin B, and part of the beta-carotene group of vitamins. In nature, it gives carrots and lobsters their distinctive orange and pink color, for example. For humans, taking a vitamin with astaxanthin can provide a range of health benefits: it acts as an antioxidant, protects from UV skin damage, and can even support cognitive health.[10] It was why Roche first commercialized it. But over time, its market evolved. More producers started offering it, turning astaxanthin into a commodity. And, remarkably, the vitamin's customer base started to morph, too, with industrial fisheries becoming a major client. They used it to give their salmon their preferred tone of pink or orange. The practice was not toxic, but it also had no relation to Roche's purpose anymore in this way. It also interfered with the natural process that created problems in industrial fishing. So, after reviewing those elements, Roche decided it made more sense to divest the business.)

With these "distractions" out of the way, Roche could fully concentrate on innovation. The company always focused on bringing innovative patient treatments to market. Now it made that pursuit official: "We innovate healthcare," was our stated goal from the early 2000s on, which later evolved to "Innovation: it's in our DNA," and finally the purpose statement we still use today: "Doing now what patients need next." (Chapter 4 has more on the origins of our purpose statement.) In all these statements, it was clear what Roche was—and what it was not. In the years that followed, this focus helped the company streamline its R&D and M&A activities. Roche went "all in," for example, on an initial investment it had made in Genentech, an innovative drug development company in the US (more on that later). It also went ahead with the integration of Boehringer Mannheim, a leading diagnostics firm in Germany. And, of course, it increased its investments in its pipeline of new drugs.

The long-term results couldn't have been better. If Roche was relatively underperforming at the time of the Novartis interest, a decade later it had surpassed Novartis in sales and market capitalization. And if the company had previously lost sight of its purpose, it was now squarely focused on it. These two elements were also inextricably linked. To be a successful participant in a capitalist economy, a company needs focus, and it needs a compass. Additionally, to have societal impact as a company, you need to be financially successful. It is a lesson Roche learned firsthand, but that most companies would do well to incorporate. That is the moral of this story.

On a personal level, the Feldmeilen process and the challenges I encountered in those early years of holding a board seat in the company may well have been the catalysts for seeing our controlling ownership of Roche as a duty and a job, as well as a privilege. With ownership came responsibility. As long-term oriented owners, we liberated the company and its management from the quarterly performance imperative that was (and sometimes still is) so prevalent. But we did need to clearly articulate to management the company's purpose, and its long-term goals, and guard over its execution. That was the "job" part of our ownership. As for the "duty": Roche's innovations for patients, its sourcing practices, and its employment of 100,000 staff members, were all incredibly powerful levers for us to have an impact on the world. But then we did need to see those "social responsibilities" as part of our duty as owners, and not just expect financial returns from our investment. Releasing our investment to support philanthropy might have been another way to act on that social responsibility, Milton Friedman might have argued. But from personal experience, I knew that philanthropy is often a short-term solution for short-term needs. Through the formative experience of the Feldmeilen process and the events that preceded it, I became and remain convinced that long-term benefits accrue from maintaining a "steady hand on the tiller" of a company. It is not how you spend your money that matters, but how you make it.

By the early 2010s, Roche had achieved success in its over-arching goals. It was delivering innovations for the next generation of patients, staff, and shareholders. But the economic system as a whole was still unsustainable, as evidenced by the great financial crisis, the destruction of nature, and ever-widening inequality. If we wanted the company to thrive for another generation—for the children of my children—we needed to do something about that. The company had to pursue a sustainable business model, and the societies it operated in needed to become more inclusive and prosperous again. It is the challenge we look at next.

Chapter 4

Roche Today

The Road to Sustainability

F or a company to thrive in the long run, it cannot just *take*. It needs to *contribute* to the societies it is part of and *regenerate* the planet it lives and depends on. That is perhaps the most straightforward definition of sustainability in a corporate context: that you give and take to such a degree, that you end up having a "net positive" impact on society and the planet (to use a term coined by former Unilever CEO Paul Polman). Entrepreneurs who start out today can use this as a design principle for their business from the start (though they will find that a lot of laws, regulations, and customs still prevent them from attaining true corporate sustainability; more on that later). But for the economy at large to become sustainable and inclusive, large, legacy businesses must change their practices, too.

How did Roche get ready for this new era? How is it positioning itself to be around for much longer, doing its share for a

---

Note to readers: the next chapters of the book either are case studies or describe the authors' concept of "the new nature of business" and are written mostly in the third person.

sustainable future for all? Those are the questions we'll attempt to answer in this chapter. The agenda André's family-controlled business followed in recent years was based on three areas: finding the right people and empowering them, fine-tuning the company's purpose and business model, and focusing on sustainability in all aspects of the organization.

Finding the Right People and Empowering Them

Every company, at its very core, is made up of people. All the money and the patents in the world are worthless if there isn't also an abundance of human and social capital. But how do you attract talented people and have them bring their best selves to their work? Roche believes it comes down to two crucial levers: having the right leaders and empowering staff at every level to live the company's values. That may sound straightforward, but it is hard in practice.

The first key personnel decision André was directly involved in was that of hiring a new CEO in 2008: Severin Schwan. The Austrian native had joined the company in 1993 as a trainee in the finance department and, after his 2008 appointment, would go on to serve 15 years as CEO before being appointed chairman in 2023. Looking back, his 30-year long tenure as an employee in many ways embodied the transition the company went through as a whole, marked by both continuity and change, and a gradual move toward sustainability.

The continuity, of course, stemmed from the fact that Severin had been with the company for 15 years before he was appointed. During that time, he had spent several years in the finance and diagnostics divisions of Roche in different parts of the world. His last role before becoming CEO was to lead the global diagnostics division. It meant that he was steeped in departments that were crucial to Roche's past and future.

For reasons mentioned previously, the finance department had gained an outsized role in the company's performance in the 1980s and 1990s. But even in Roche's more-focused business model, finance would continue to have a vital control function going forward. Indeed, balancing long-term investments, short-term costs, and value-based pricing is crucial for a company like Roche. It was good to have someone with direct knowledge of these financial considerations at the head of the company. Severin's experience in the diagnostics division, meanwhile, was critical for another reason: the development of "personalized health care," in which treatments are tailored to patients based on their individual diagnosis, was quickly becoming the unique value proposition of the company. Roche was the first in the industry to offer highly specific diagnostics tests, which could in a next phase of treatment be paired with highly effective and personalized medicines. If it was going to be able to deliver on its purpose of "doing now what patients need next," then a fine-tuned and state-of-the-art diagnostics division was of the essence.

In an interview with us for this book, Severin talked about how the feeling of stability and continuity at the top helped him and others do his job for the long run: "I was the seventh CEO in 125 years, and that has a lot to do with the ownership structure of Roche" he said. "Normally if you have a crisis, the CEO is quick to be fired by shareholders. It's like in a football club, where the manager gets sacked when there are a few bad results. Working for a family-controlled company is different because [the family] *looks through* the cycle of innovation."

But Severin also represented change. When he started at the company, personalized health care was still in its infancy (in fact, the actual collaboration between the pharmaceuticals and diagnostics divisions was still rather limited, Severin noted). The concept of sustainability was similarly underdeveloped. Under his tenure, however, Roche's purpose statement of "doing now what patients need next" became explicit and got to have a concrete meaning. The company also started its journey toward sustainability in earnest, putting it on a path to being net positive toward people and the planet. Let's look at those two aspects of Roche's transformation next.

Fine-Tuning the Purpose: "Doing Now What Patients Need Next"

For a company to have a positive impact on society, it needs to articulate what its purpose is in the world and find a business model that backs it up. At Roche, the implicit notion that the company wanted to "do now what patients need next" was present since time immemorial. The transformational challenge was to make it the foundation of *everything* Roche did. (As we saw previously, for some time, some noncore activities had guided decision-making as well.) After the failed takeover attempt of Roche by Novartis, the company became laser focused on that challenge.

Focusing on this core meant, for example, that the R&D investments across the group steadily grew from 8.8 billion Swiss francs per year in 2008 (about $9.8 billion)[1] to 14 billion Swiss francs ($15.6 billion) in 2022,[2] representing more than a fifth of the company's overall revenues. Innovation also became the singular leitmotif for Roche's M&A activity. One of the new top management's first major milestones was to fully acquire the California-based Genentech, a biotechnology pioneer, for almost $47 billion.[3] (Roche had previously held a majority stake.) It is worth a closer look.

Since its founding in 1976, Genentech had taken a novel approach to innovating health care. It got its start in genetic engineering technology,[5] hence Genentech, and more specifically in a technique called *recombinant DNA*. What that meant, in short, was that the company identified small pieces of biological DNA that could help cure a disease, isolated and grew them, and then turned them into a highly precise medicine for specific patients.

Roche and Genentech, a Long Joint History

The long-standing ties between Roche and the San Francisco–based Genentech had their origins in both companies' pioneering efforts in the biotechnology space, Roche historian Alexander Bieri told us. On the Roche side, the Roche Institute for Molecular Biology, founded in 1968 at the company's facilities in Nutley, New Jersey, was one of the cradles of the industry, funding groundbreaking scientific innovations of geneticists. Anna-Marie Skalka, for example, developed trailblazing techniques for recombinant genetic engineering there, and Sidney Pestka, who later received the National Medal of Technology, isolated human interferon. (An interferon is a natural substance that helps the body's immune system fight infection and other diseases, such as cancer.[4]) Their work was also the reason why Roche contacted Genentech as early as 1978, barely 20 months after Genentech's foundation, Bieri added. Two years later, the two companies signed a collaboration agreement, which enabled them to jointly develop the process for manufacturing interferon, which would go on to help patients around the world in the decades following. The product was launched by Roche as its first fully biotechnologically produced medicine in 1986 as Roferon-A. When the milestone payments of Roche to Genentech ended, however, Genentech came into a tight spot because of upcoming expensive clinical trials. Under the leadership of Chairman Fritz Gerber, Roche took over 60% of the stock of Genentech in 1990.

The company's technique of putting biology, not chemistry, at the heart of pharmaceutical innovation, was so novel it gave birth to an entirely new industry: biotech. Its culture was novel, too, being described internally as one of "casual intensity." What mattered in this approach was the fundamental research and breakthroughs its employees came up with, not the hierarchy they were part of, or any buttoned-up suits they wore. Genentech was, to

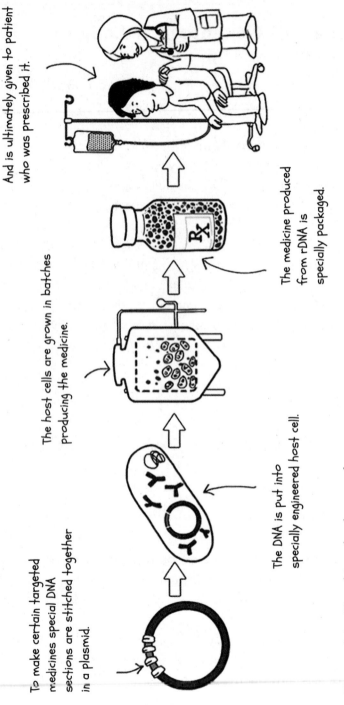

To make certain targeted medicines special DNA sections are stitched together in a plasmid.

The DNA is put into specially engineered host cell.

The host cells are grown in batches producing the medicine.

The medicine produced from rDNA is specially packaged.

And is ultimately given to patient who was prescribed it.

Figure 4.1 How biotechnology works.

Source: Genentech, Biotech Basics.

make a comparison, more akin to a Silicon Valley tech company than the more "old-world, staid, suit-and-tie" culture of Roche,[6] as one observer put it.

But combining the culture of both companies worked. Some of the best elements of both Roche and Genentech found their way to the other, while each also kept their unique identity. Roche had a more formal style, for example, but it was also dedicated to a "devolved" type of management. It is organized on the principle of subsidiarity, meaning there was a high degree of independence for local management at various subsidiaries. (This approach has also been a key success factor in Roche's alliance with Chugai, its majority-controlled entity in Japan.) Genentech's model, however, was very explicit in its focus on patients, which was an inspiration for Roche. When you entered the campus in South San Francisco, Severin said, you saw huge posters on the facade of buildings showing patients who benefitted from Genentech medicines. Patients were regularly invited to staff meetings, and the corridors were plastered with patient testimonials. "When asked what Genentech is about, nearly every employee, be it the receptionist or a scientist in the lab, would talk first and foremost about making a difference for patients," Severin told us. It was a result of the Genentech acquisition, he said, that an explicit purpose statement for the entire Roche Group was codified—with the patient at its very core.

Roche Purpose Statement: Doing Now What Patients Need Next

We believe it's urgent to deliver medical solutions right now—even as we develop innovations for the future. We are passionate about transforming patients' lives. We are courageous in both decision and action. And we believe that good business means a better world.

(continued)

(continued)

That is why we come to work each day. We commit ourselves to scientific rigor, unassailable ethics, and access to medical innovations for all. We do this today to build a better tomorrow.

We are proud of who we are, what we do, and how we do it. We are many, working as one across functions, across companies, and across the world.

We are Roche.

Sustainability at Roche

Perhaps the biggest change that occurred under Roche's new management was to start the journey to become a "sustainable" business. It started with management and staff getting to know the concept, which had *not* been a part of anyone's curriculum or job function before. As Severin told us in an interview for this book, "there were a lot of reasons why I joined Roche as a trainee in 1993. But sustainability was not one of them. I'm not sure I even knew the word."

As time went by, though, a sustainability mindset started to enter the company culture, both from the top down and from the bottom up. "It started at Roche with Luc Hoffmann," Severin said, "but over time the topic of sustainability became exponentially important across society as a whole, from not at all to very important. For example, in job interviews, candidates are nowadays asking about the purpose of the company, about how to save the world. When I started in the early nineties, people would have suspected that you just tried to please them with such questions. It would have been regarded as pseudo-altruistic. But today, if the company doesn't genuinely care about these topics and has no good answers, new employees will not be interested to join."

The fact that Roche is serious about sustainability doesn't mean that the concept is rigidly defined, though. There is a recognition at the company that "corporate sustainability" in today's economic system is still often a contradiction. To change that, and give true meaning to sustainability, Roche's follows the Chinese philosophy of "crossing the river by touching the stones": it is implemented step-by-step and with a focus on stability.

Sustainability: A Definition

For the United Nations, sustainability means "meetings the needs of the present without compromising the ability of future generations to meet their own needs."[7] It was a definition articulated by the "Brundtland commission" of the United Nations, which convened in 1987 under the leadership of Chairwoman Gro Harlem Brundtland, a former Norwegian prime minister.[8] The report kicked off the modern movement toward sustainability globally, and directly led to the seminal 1989 UN Conference on Environment and Development and the 1992 UN Earth Summit.

Today, the multilateral sustainability agenda at the UN lives on in the so-called Conference of the Parties (COPs). There are COPs on climate change, biodiversity, desertification, and other topics. But the most well-known, without a doubt, are those on climate change. Most readers will have heard about the Kyoto Protocol, for example, agreed at the COP on climate change in Kyoto, Japan, from 1997, or the Paris Agreement, resulting from the climate COP in 2016. The most recent climate COPs are those that took place in Glasgow, UK (2021), Sharm El-Sheikh, Egypt (2022), and Dubai, UAE (2023). Increasingly, however, the COP on biodiversity is gaining notoriety and interest, too, as the realization grows that sustainability is not just about climate but also about nature more broadly. The most

(continued)

(continued)

notable COPs in biodiversity were those in Aichi, Japan, in 2010, which led to the Aichi Targets on biodiversity, and more recently the Kunming/Montreal COP (2022), which led to the global target of being "nature positive" by 2030.

Despite the recent engagement of business on the sidelines of these meetings, the COP processes work mainly through multilateral processes and government action. That makes sense: sustainability at its core is a macro concept that has a meaning only on a global scale. It is hard for any one person or company to label themselves as sustainable. Yet, sustainability needs to have a concrete meaning for individual businesses. Otherwise, a company cannot know whether what it does helps or hurts system-wide sustainability. Despite the increased attention the concept has received in recent years, though, this challenge has eluded the business and academic world.

In the past few years, Roche has adopted a pragmatic approach. "Sustainability is a lot about the net value we provide to society," Severin told us. On the one hand, "our gross contribution is the delivery of innovative medical solutions for people around the world, which needs a lot of creativity and stamina along the way." In this regard, Severin also pointed out that it is essential for Roche to receive appropriate compensation for its solutions and does not simply provide them free of charge, even if it has the goal of expanding access as widely as possible. Ultimately, the billions of dollars Roche invests in research and development at high risk need to be earned back so Roche can sustain itself financially.

On the other hand, to find out whether Roche delivers a net positive value to society, Severin emphasized, it also needs to account for the pollution of the environment it causes, or any damage it does to the social tissue of society. It is this cost, which adds to the conventional financial ones, that it wants to account for before it can claim to be "sustainable." As indicated, that challenge has so far eluded the business world because many of the externalities caused by companies do not have a market value or even an assigned societal value. But it hasn't stopped the company from starting where it can. It led to a series of sustainability efforts that are both top-down, and bottom-up. Let us highlight three.

Product Stewardship

One good example of that top-down, bottom-up approach to sustainability is an area called *product stewardship,*[9] a concept Roche uses for its diagnostics instruments and solutions. For Roche engaging in product stewardship means that the company aims to minimize the (negative) health, safety, environmental and social impacts of its products. It may sound a bit vague as a starting point, but it has very practical consequences in real life. It means, for example, that product designers will think of the waste their products create at the end user level, and alleviate this waste upfront by designing the product differently. And, because Roche makes many products, product stewardship has been a core element of Roche's sustainability strategy, Richeal Cline and David Trindell told us in an interview for this book. (Richeal is global head of quality, regulatory, and product stewardship at Roche Diagnostics, based in Indianapolis, Indiana. David is Roche's vice president of corporate environment, health, and safety, based in South San Francisco, California.) One of Roche's 10-year ambitions is to reduce the company's total environmental impact by half, and another is to double patient access to high–medical value diagnostics solutions. (Other 10-year ambitions of Roche will be highlighted in Chapter 6.) They each affect sustainability in their own way:

- *Doubling patient access to high–medical value diagnostics solutions* is about increasing Roche's positive societal contribution.

- *Reducing the environmental impact by half*[10] is about Roche's efforts do less harm to the environment and make an environmental contribution.

Note: many companies nowadays have objectives for their environmental impact, particularly when it comes to carbon emissions; about half of the largest global companies have a so-called net-zero carbon emissions target,[11] most often for 2050. But these plans often do not pass muster when scrutinized. According to Net Zero Tracker, an organization that assesses the quality of net-zero pledges made by companies, "only 4% of company net zero commitments meet the revised 'Starting Line criteria,' set out by the UN Race to Zero campaign."[12] Companies often fail on any of the following litmus tests: setting a specific net-zero target, covering all greenhouse gases (including so-called indirect, or Scope 3, emissions, which cover the emissions from suppliers or customers), setting clear conditions for the use of offsets, publishing a plan, implementing immediate emission-cutting measures, or doing annual progress reporting.

That kind of ambiguity has been absent at Roche. There is not just a net-zero, but a real zero, goal on carbon emissions for 2050.[13] What that means is that Roche would rather not rely on carbon offsets, but prefers to reduce its *absolute* emissions, whether from products, offices, or travel.[14] Roche has also set clear intermediary CO_2 emissions reduction objectives for 2025 and 2029—40% and 75%, respectively, Annual progress reports keep track of all of Roche's areas of performance, including "indirect" emissions from sourcing or using Roche products.[15]

It is also not just carbon emissions that Roche has been working on, but its entire environmental footprint. In 2017, the company was one of the first to make a "natural capital protocol pilot study."[16] It showed the impacts and dependencies of Roche on society and the environment and translated those impacts into a monetary value. About 80% of the negative impact Roche generated at the time was due to greenhouse gas emissions. But the other

20% also mattered: it included other air pollution (9.3%), other impact from travel (7.6%), and noise from travel (1.4%). In a sign of how far the company had come since the 1970s, water use and discharges (1.1%), incineration from chemical waste (0.4%) and incineration from nonhazardous waste (0.2%) had fallen way off the list of top negative environmental impacts. It was a great help in refining Roche's product stewardship goals down the line.

Bottom-Up Initiatives

The key to achieving great ambitions, in this case on environmental impact, has always been to empower staff at all levels of the organization. It is not in the board room that environmental impacts are reduced. It is in the labs and the production facilities, on the roads, and in patient clinics. A few examples from Richeal and David prove the point. Take the reduction in environmental impact of a given diagnostics test, such as a pregnancy test or a cancer diagnosis. Already in the feasibility and development phase of a new product, important questions need to be answered, Richeal said. "How do we produce the test? How much energy and water are needed? What does packaging look like? What kind of bottle does it go in?" And even more questions arise in the production and logistics phase. "How does the test get distributed? Can we ship it at room temperature? How can we make sure there is sustainable supply?" The answers to those questions come from researchers, designers, plant managers, purchase managers, and other people "in the trenches" of the organization.

The devil is sometimes in the detail. One team recently came up with a way to reduce the environmental impact of a user manual, by going from a saddle-stitched one, to a foldable one. A simple idea, but one that would cost 70% less, and reduce the environmental impact of the manual by almost half (48%). It required not just coming up with the bright idea, but getting government approval for it, as the product was FDA regulated. It passed. Another innovation, in a pharmaceutical product, was to fit four injectors in the same sized box, instead of two, while making the product both disposable, and recyclable, where previously it had not been. The reduced packaging in turn had a knock-on effect on transport, as fewer and smaller shipments of the product were needed. Finally, for one test, the product team was able to decrease the blood sample size needed, which in turn led to a lower volume of water (36%) needed for every test. Many of these small improvements and innovations add up to achieving the next year's goal. And sharing them as best practices across the company, with other teams, is what allows for company-wide leaps forward over time.

If you want people to feel empowered to come up with such sustainable innovations, it matters that they know these efforts are rewarded and appreciated. When Richeal was working in the US in the 2010s, knowing that André, as vice-chairman, was supportive of sustainability measures was a reason for her to get ahead of the curve on the use of refrigerants in Roche's cooling systems, she told us. "I led a facility in New Jersey, and we had the board [of directors] come to visit," she told us. "I gave a presentation to the board, and the first question I got was from André, asking if we were 'K6' compliant. Thankfully we were able to answer 'yes' at the time. My exposure in this topic, in this career, has been tightly connected with André's passion in the space," she concluded.

The specific directive Richeal referred to here was an internal but company-wide directive on the elimination of halogenic refrigerants. In the late 1980s already, these refrigerants, often used in air-conditioning systems, were proven to contribute to ozone depletion, and cause other environmental harms. As a result, Roche had started to limit their use and source alternatives. But the cooling systems were still very much in use in the US years later because the country didn't have any strict government regulation. It meant that Roche employees there had to go against the stream. In doing so, they often encountered sourcing issues because the regulatory framework and market conditions weren't favorable.

Knowing that it would make them compliant to an internal directive was one motivator for Roche's US personnel to forge ahead anyway. But having the backing of the management and the board, clearly, was another.

David pointed to another benefit of working for Roche on sustainability: "The fact that Roche is family-controlled [means] it can have an agenda that is not driven by next quarterly financial statement," he told us. "[As an employee], it gives a general sense of having greater flexibility to be longer-term in your thinking." One example he cited was in the choice of the type of energy used for product manufacturing. To decide on its investments, his team usually does a "net present value" calculation on various alternatives. But unlike other companies, he said, "[our team] was allowed to go with a longer-term discount cost, because there wasn't this kind of [short-term] pressure." It has often made investing in a renewable source of energy viable before it has been the case for other companies. "It was different from rest of industry," he said. "It is this longer-term visibility, because we are going to be around [for a long time], and we can wait that time to recoup those investments."

The Roche Buildings in Basel

Arguably the most visible element of Roche's increased commitment to sustainability is its new corporate headquarters in Basel, including two skyscrapers that function as offices, as well as an adjoining research facility, known as pRED center (short for *pharma Research and Early Development*). These Roche buildings, the last of which was finished in 2023, are state-of-the art in terms of energy efficiency, construction materials, and integration of environmental elements. Today, the towers stand tall over the city. At 205 and 178 meters (673 and 584 feet), they are the tallest buildings in Switzerland.[17] But in 2007, as the project was about to kick off, it was almost shelved at the last minute.

The original design of the Roche Towers, conceived in the early 2000s, was a real eye-catcher. The headquarters was imagined as a gigantic spiral, representing the DNA helix that symbolizes many of the Roche biomedicines (see Figure 4.2). But as the design got reviewed by the board and the family shareholders, they felt as though the splashy design wasn't blending in well with the city of Basel and its people. Basel is not about showing off, they felt. It is about doing good, but not talking about it. "It has a lot to do with the Calvinistic culture," Severin told us. In times of religious persecutions in Europe, Calvinists, and later also Jews, came to Basel. By the late 19th century, the city was a haven of freedom in an otherwise turbulent Europe. "Immigrants came to the city, and adapted, but didn't want to be loud," he said. "They gave a lot

Figure 4.2   A rendering of the first design of the new Roche headquarters.

Source: with permission of SECONEA.

of money, but in a very humble, modest way." That was the Basel that Fritz Hoffmann, the founder of Roche, had grown up in, and this spirit is still present today. Soon after Severin took over as CEO, the board pulled the plug on the original design. Roche still wanted to build its new headquarters, and it still deemed a high riser the most appropriate way to do so. But the DNA helix was dropped. It was too much of a head turner, and that didn't fit with the city's identity.

Nevertheless, the need for new headquarters in the city remained high. As the company had expanded over the decades, its employees had been placed in an ever-increasing number of offices spread throughout the city. You could often see employees crisscrossing the city on foot to get from one meeting to another. It had its charms, but hurt overall collaboration, and many of the older buildings didn't meet the latest energy efficiency standards, either. The company's main goal going forward was to bring everyone back together in central, modern offices; its second aim was to do so in a way that caused as little damage to the environment as possible. Roche didn't want to have a sprawling campus outside the city, where people had to commute to by car, with huge parking lots, and an enormous horizontal footprint. It wanted to remain in the city, take up as little space as possible, and maintain the social fabric of being in an urban area. Finally, the company wanted to blend in with the city's culture and heritage. The local Basel architect bureau Herzog & de Meuron, was trusted with coming up with architecture that was in line with the times, and in line with the identity of the city. In a meeting with the architects, Severin told them what the assignment came down to: "The goal is that this building is invisible," he said. "That was the direction we had to go for."

The architects had grown up around Basel's Peter Rot-Strasse themselves, literally a stone's throw away from the new headquarters, so they had affinity with the neighborhood and its people. With the new briefing, the architects quickly came up with the new and final design. The buildings they designed would still stand tall but they would no longer stand out. The buildings would have a white, misty color, so they would blend in with the clouds and seem to disappear in the sky. They would also be narrower at the top, a bit like a pyramid, so their appearance wouldn't be as oppressive. And their glass would be partially light absorbing, which would make the towers blur with their environment. The new towers would be more like the city: influential, but in a subdued way. (See Figure 4.3.)

The other challenge, of course, was to make the new head-quarters environmentally sustainable. It was made possible by a variety of efforts. Much of the heating and cooling of the building, for example, is done with the help of groundwater. In addition to

Figure 4.3   Roche's new headquarters as seen from a nearby street in Basel.

Source: with permission of F. Hoffmann-La Roche Ltd.

state-of-the-art isolation techniques, it means the building is near energy independent, and near zero in terms of carbon emissions. To access the building, sustainability ranked high on the agenda, too. Located in the very center of the city, most employees can commute by train, tram, or bicycle to the company. A large underground parking for bicycles ensures their centrality as mobility mode of choice. (Even esthetically, many of the choices are inspired by nature. The large entrance halls feature hanging gardens, giving visitors and employees the feeling of being in a natural environment. The carpets in the building are almost all made of recycled fishing nets.) The towers express the vision Roche has for sustainability: one where the human impact on the environment is minimal and where emissions are reduced in absolute terms, not by relying on offsets.

At the pRED center, the last of the new Roche buildings to be finished, another sustainable building technique was possible: the recycling of construction demolition waste. Thanks to the latest innovations, rather than throwing away the (cement and concrete) waste from the buildings that had previously stood where the new pRED center would rise, much of this old material could be recycled into the new concrete. The center was literally built with stones of its predecessors, a bit like how ancient Romans and medieval peoples had gone about construction. The approach was a novelty, made possibly only through innovation, because in most of the world, including the US and Switzerland, recycling old concrete was until recently not allowed by building codes because of safety concerns. In the Roche case, the owner, construction firms, and building material companies involved all worked together to come up with a solution that met both safety and sustainability standards. With concrete being one of the greatest sources of CO_2 emissions in the world, this approach was also a great environmental success. It has been since applied elsewhere in Switzerland, where it is now allowed by law if safety criteria are met, as well as in other pioneering countries. (You can read more on that in Chapter 7.)

★ ★ ★

At 125 years, Roche has been sustainable in at least one sense. From Fritz Hoffmann-La Roche to some of André's nephews' and nieces' children, already six generations of Hoffmanns, Oeris, and Duschmalés (the family names of the current branches of the family) have seen the family company prosper. But to display sustainable leadership today, it is necessary to look several generations into the future once again.

Roche has already set several sustainability goals for 2050, including on carbon emissions,[18] which constitute the most imminent risk for an unsustainable future. The company's current goal is to issue *zero* carbon by 2050. It is an ambitious goal, not yet achievable at scale with the current state of technology. Yet it would be much better still if this *real zero* target were achieved much sooner than 2050, André believes. It is why it was so important the company set ambitious milestones for earlier dates, too, validated by the Science Based Targets initiative[19] at the end of 2022, and in line with the UN goal of limiting global warming to 1.5 degrees Celsius. Roche's new headquarters is also future proof and will likely stand for at least a century or more. Finally, the company's business model has gotten an update to be relevant deep into the 21st century, with the aim of "doing now what patients need next."

But as important as these goals and accomplishments are, much more work remains to be done. For one, the company needs to shift its focus from climate alone to nature more broadly and operate a business ecosystem within planetary boundaries. Roche—like the whole business world—needs to see nature as an ally, and not just as a problem. For any forward-thinking company, the next step is to set science-based targets for *nature*, in addition to climate targets. At Roche, that step is underway. It will start with externally validated nature targets, and end with embedding them into the remuneration of corporate leadership. Society, too, needs an economic system that finds a better balance between rewarding innovation and progress on the one hand and allowing broad-based prosperity on the other. More than anything, perhaps, there is a need for business leaders who also act as societal leaders, thinking through the consequences of their actions and strategies on society at large. These are the challenges we will tackle in the next chapters of this book.

Chapter 5

The Roots of the New Nature of Business

Whereas Thomas More published *Utopia* in 1516, his description of the fabled island was both fiction and nonfiction. It was fiction, of course, because Utopia never existed and never would materialize. *Utopia* literally means "no place" in Greek, and everything about it was entirely made up. But in some other ways, Utopia was real. It was a sign of a mindset change already underway in Europe at the time. The Utopian island that More described was allegedly set off the coast of the New World, which had in fact just been discovered a few years earlier. It was governed by humanistic, pluralistic, and quasi-democratic principles, which would make their way in parts of Europe and the Americas, in the decades and centuries to come (though often only after a lot of strife, bloodshed, and discrimination). And some of the most unbelievable features of Utopia, such as its welfare system, or the fact that people worked only six hours a day, became a reality in some parts of the world many generations later, or are finally on the horizon today.[a]

If you are a critic of Utopia, don't worry. We don't bring the book up because we see More's 500-year-old imagined island society as an ideal today. We bring it up because the vision we have for business and society also has some features that may seem far-fetched today, but are just around the corner. Equally, some features may be out of reach for now, but could become plausible in the next few decades if we lay the groundwork today. And in any case, the ideas we believe in are ones we hope most people could get behind and that are therefore worth pursuing in and of themselves. So here goes. If there is an ideal system to organize society and our economy today, it would include these characteristics: the protection of nature, the pursuit of broad-based prosperity, and the respect of democracy and fundamental human rights. If these characteristics become the basis of our system, we believe, they will lead to *lasting prosperity for all*. It's not as catchy as *Utopia*, perhaps, but a worthy goal to strive for, just as much.

This system of sustainable, inclusive prosperity is possible, but it is not the one we are living in today. At best, we achieved parts of its equation. A capitalist economy that encourages innovation, for example, is still in place in many of the world's largest economies. It has created tremendous wealth and prosperity, but in an increasingly unequal way.[b] The world is also home to many vibrant democracies, but the arc of history is no longer bending toward them, and the quality of most democracies is declining. In fact, according to the Stockholm-based Institute for Democracy and Electoral Assistance, "half of democratic governments around

---

[a] In fairness, some other features of Utopia are still outlandish today, or have become so over time. Utopia approved of slavery, for example, albeit mostly as a form of punishment. Utopia also presented communistic life as an ideal, because there was no private property and meals were shared in dining halls. And finally, though progressive for the time, the position of the woman was abominable from today's point of view.

[b] That in turn led to a whole set of other problems, including frustrations and revolt among those who do not have what they deserve, and futile investment and consumption choices made by those who have more than their fair share.

the world are in decline, undermined by problems ranging from restrictions on freedom of expression to distrust in the legitimacy of elections."[1] Despite their shortcomings, we should cherish both capitalism and democracy. They are the systems that brought the world prosperity and peace, even if they are urgently in need of an upgrade.

When it comes to protection of nature, however, the picture is one-sidedly and decidedly bleak. We are truly headed toward dystopia. Since André was a teenager more than 60% of all the vertebrated species have gone extinct,[2] to cite just one stark statistic. It sadly illustrates the larger planetary crisis we are living through, and of which the climate crisis is only the most pressing. We have been warned about this crisis for generations, but unfortunately, we have not done much about it—not as democratic societies and not as business ecosystems. We've consistently pretended that nature and business are two separate things.

Yet all human activity, including business activity, very much depends on and affects nature (see Figure 5.1).

On the one hand, nature provides businesses with all kinds of ecosystem services, which companies in turn use to provide products and services to society. Think of Apple using all kinds of metals and rare earth elements, for example, to produce its iPhones, or a construction materials firm using limestone to produce cement and concrete. On the other hand, business affects nature, both directly and indirectly, by producing waste and pollution, for example, but also if it restores the sites it exploits to let them rewild or regenerate (though this is still a rather rare practice).

In the early 1970s, scientists of the Club of Rome first rang the alarm bell on this interdependency, warning that we had reached "the limits to growth."[c] Our model of ever-expanding industrial

---

[c] "Published 1972—The message of this book still holds today: The earth's interlocking resources—the global system of nature in which we all live—probably cannot support present rates of economic and population growth much beyond the year 2100, if that long, even with advanced technology."—text taken from the description of "The Limits to Growth" on The Club of Rome website, accessed February 15, 2024, https://www.clubofrome.org/publication/the-limits-to-growth/.

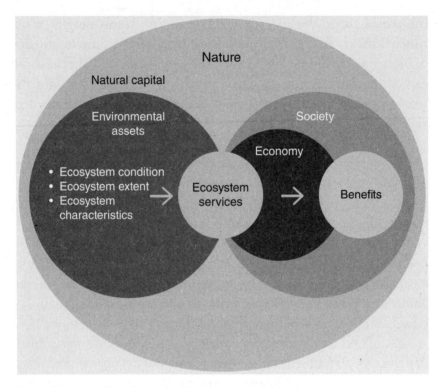

Figure 5.1   How nature, business, and society interact.

Source: Recommendations of the Taskforce on Nature-Related Financial Disclosures, 2023 / TNFD / CC BY 4.0.

and demographic development could lead to an environmental (and economic) breakdown, they predicted. Today, we must acknowledge that the warnings of the Club of Rome were largely right.[3] (Note: André is a member of the organization.) In 2018, researchers from Stockholm University updated the predictions from the club and came to the sobering conclusion that "most of the 'Limits to Growth' original conclusions still hold true."[4] In 2023, they updated their research to include nine specific "planetary boundaries" within which we must remain to sustain our life on earth. Six out of these nine had been crossed, with three of those transgressions occurring in just the past 15 years (see Figure 5.2). "We don't know how long we can keep transgressing

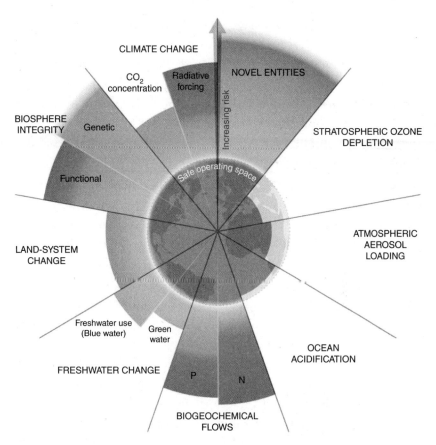

Figure 5.2   The 2023 update to the planetary boundaries.
Source: Stockholm Resilience Centre.

these key boundaries before combined pressures lead to irreversible change and harm," Johan Rockström, the lead author of the study, and currently director of the Potsdam Institute for Climate Impact Research, commented.[5]

What becomes crystal clear from these kinds of studies is that we are living on a planet with finite resources, and that its limits are becoming ever-more apparent. The mass burning of fossil fuels, which leads to an increased concentration of CO_2 in the air, and causes climate change, is the most obvious and egregious element of this unsustainable system, but it is nowhere near the only one.

Some of the damage we have caused, such as the destruction of wildlife habitats, or the change in freshwater or plastic pollutants, will take generations to repair. Other damage is irreversible, as species that have gone extinct won't ever come back. Clearly, we have not seen business taking on a new nature on a global scale, or we would not find ourselves in this situation.

When it comes to world's social and human capital, too, we're headed in the wrong direction. For a relatively short period of time, broadly between the 1950s and the early 1980s, many Western societies had a "social compact" in place which propelled them forward, leaving ever fewer people behind. Its foundations were the "welfare state" in Western Europe, or the "Great Society" in the US. They included, depending on the country, policies such as social security, guaranteed public health care, access to education, and worker protections, such as the freedom to unionize and negotiate labor contracts. One result of this social compact was that companies could tap into a wealth of social and human capital. Another was that economic inequality went down, and the middle class in these countries became the backbone of the economy.

That is no longer the society many of us live in today. In the world's most prosperous nation, the United States, income and wealth inequality have soared to levels often not seen in almost a century.[6] Public health care and education are under immense pressure, both financially and in terms of their quality, leading to fewer pathways to success and health for many families. The sad phenomenon, known as *deaths of despair*, is on the rise.[7] (Deaths of despair is "a collective term for deaths from alcohol, drugs and suicide, which tend to occur much more frequently in socially deprived communities," as per the University of Manchester.[8]) And unions are on the backfoot almost universally, too, leading in some instances to wages and worker rights more reminiscent of the Gilded Age of the late 19th century than that of the Golden Age of capitalism in the second half of the 20th century.

The reasons for this worrying evolution are multiple and complex. One reason is that some of the technological innovations that spread in recent decades *replaced* workers by automating their work, rather than *augmenting* their skills. Think of sales personnel in retail stores and supermarkets, tellers in banks, or even accountants doing bookkeeping. Another reason is the advance of globalization and unfettered free trade. Looking at globalization from a global GDP perspective, its effect has been uniquely positive. In some major emerging economies such as China, India, Indonesia, or Vietnam, globalization also enabled people to climb out of poverty and into the middle class. But free trade as we know it has also had major downsides. It caused increased financial volatility in turbulent times (though it is also found to reduce volatility in tranquil times).[9] It enabled multinational companies to record earnings in jurisdictions where they could minimize their tax bill (as opposed to recording them where they occurred)[10]—at least until a global minimum tax came into effect in 2024.[11] And, in countries such as the US, but also European countries, it destroyed local jobs in manufacturing,[12] shipping them overseas instead. This social and economic inequality itself, moreover, has been a root cause for the further degradation of other capitals.

But despite these worrying evolutions we *can* create a system of sustainable prosperity going forward, of that we are convinced. For companies, it requires adopting a *new nature of business*. This consists of three crucial elements, very much like the main parts of a tree: the roots, the trunk, and the crown. In this comparison, the new nature of business looks as follows:

- **The roots: regenerate nature.** Put an end to harmful and pollutive economic activities, and replace them with the practice of working with nature, not against it.
- **The trunk: build with intent.** Reflect on your corporate purpose, set goals that go beyond profits, and measure and disclose all your impacts and dependencies.
- **The crown: lead and let lead.** Let 1,000 branches grow. Empower fellow leaders to step forward, recognize the value of democracy and society, and keep a moral compass.

Lead and Let Lead

Build with Intent

Regenerate Nature

Figure 5.3   The roots, trunk, and crown of the new nature of business.
Source: Orlando Florin Rosu / Adobe Stock Photos.

In this chapter, we'll look at the roots of this new nature of business. In the next, we'll cover the trunk and the crown. (See Figure 5.3.)

The Roots: Regenerate Nature

Put an end to harmful and pollutive activities, and replace them with the practice of working with nature, not against it.

Business cannot work against nature. Unsustainable and harmful extraction and pollution should be the exception for business activity, not the rule as they are today. That is not only a matter of morality or beliefs but also one of natural logic. Just like a tree cannot grow or even survive without deep roots in a healthy soil, so the business world cannot thrive if it undercuts its own roots and pollutes the soil it is built in.

The case against harmful extraction and pollution is clearest against hydrocarbon fuels such as coal, oil, and gas. They should be phased out immediately because of the tremendous harm their burning does to life on earth and because there is no excuse not to.

Contrary to what certain corporate lobbying might make us believe, phasing out fossil fuels is a no-brainer. It should be at or near the top of the list of any business leader's or policymaker's agenda. Consider first that there is no excuse not to. Thanks to its unique place in the solar system, our planet has an abundance of all kinds of renewable energy, which are increasingly easy to harvest. Where we live, for instance, there is plenty of water and wood. In many other places, it is wind, or sun, that is omnipresent. In yet other places, it is geothermic energy.

Take the example of Switzerland. Much of the country could be supplied with renewable energy from within its own borders. In 2022, 80% of its electricity supply came from renewable sources,[13] with hydropower providing the lion's share and biomass energy a second supporter. And in a sign of how quickly change can come about, the share of renewables shot up 4% in just two years.[14] Of course, electricity is itself only a small part of most countries' total energy supply today, with the bulk still coming from oil and gas. But there really isn't any reason why having an almost exclusively "green" energy supply wouldn't be possible. Some countries are already showing the way. Iceland, for example, gets almost two-thirds of its energy from geothermal sources, and a total of 85% of its total energy supply from renewable sources.[15] Or consider Brazil. The country has historically had a lot of hydropower, and in just seven years it installed 30 gigawatts of photovoltaic energy capacity, bringing the share of solar power to about 7% in the country's electricity mix.[16] Wherever in the world renewable energy sources progress, it is thanks to companies and governments making a deliberate choice to work with nature, rather than against it.

The benefits that come from a short, localized supply chain, moreover, outweigh their costs. Electrifying the grid, and getting energy from renewable sources, helps security of supply, increases energy independency, and raises local prosperity because money is not siphoned off abroad. The system instead creates a link between people and the nature that surrounds us.

Crucially, when it comes to wind and solar energy, the technologies on the market today are already cost competitive with other sources of energy, such as fossil fuels.[17] The international renewable energy agency calculated that the global weighted average cost of electricity from solar photovoltaics fell to less than a nickel ($0.049) per kilowatt-hour, almost one-third less than the cheapest fossil fuel globally. For onshore wind, prices fell to 3 cents ($0.033) per kilowatt-hour in 2022, slightly less than half that of the cheapest fossil fuel–fired option.[18] It is a reality that was unthinkable even a decade ago, and that proves that innovation and determination can make up for most of the barriers we find in our way.

You may wonder: with renewables being so cost competitive, why are we still using fossil fuels at all? The fossil fuel industry may have you believe it is because of security of supply or the unworkable fluctuations in the supply of energy from sources such as wind and solar. These are certainly challenges that need addressing. But they are not the real reason for fossil fuels' continued dominance, because solutions for them exist. Moreover, oil and gas have their own challenges in security of supply, either because they come from unstable source countries themselves, such as Russia, Iraq, or Iran, or because they must pass through narrow sea lanes that are vulnerable to attacks. The reason for fossil fuels' continued dominance, then, is the vested interests many actors in the global economy still have in the status quo. For evidence, look no further than the fossil fuel subsidies that are still handed out around the world. The International Monetary Fund estimated there are about $1 trillion in annual explicit subsidies globally, and another

$6 trillion in "implicit" subsidies, where neither producers nor consumers bear the cost to society and the planet of the fossil fuels they produce or consume.[19] At the current rate of "progress," this total sum of subsidies will barely decline until 2030, mostly because of the absence of actions again implicit subsidies.

But even if it wasn't such a no-brainer, the immense damage that the burning of fossil fuels causes is a good enough reason to strive for other sources of energy as soon as possible. As James Gentizon, an engineer and entrepreneur André works with in Switzerland (and whom you'll meet in Chapter 8) puts it, burning fossil fuels is the "lazy" option for humanity. When we take coal and oil out of the ground, we pay nothing, except perhaps a licensing fee to the current government. The material itself is not paid for because there is no contracting party on the other side but not because these materials have no value, or indeed, cost. We are using these resources as if they are free, but of course they are not: it took the earth *hundreds of millions of years* to turn wood and other biowaste into coal and oil, only for humanity to then burn it all up in a matter of a few short hundreds of years, mostly since the industrial revolution. It makes the burning of fossil fuels unsustainable from a consumption perspective alone already because future generations won't have millions of years to spare to foresee in their energy independence. Humanity hasn't been around for as long as it took to create coal and oil in the first place.

In addition, the burning of fossil fuels is also simply incredibly harmful to our lifestyle today. By now, it has become not just scientifically proven but also a matter of lived experience that climate change is real, that it is severe, and that it has consequences in everything from global warming to extreme weather events to seasonal disruptions of the climate. You don't need to imagine what is happening in faraway places, such as the Pacific islands that are disappearing or the Arctic ice that is melting. You can find evidence much closer to home, whether you live in the US, Europe, or Asia.

The Impact of Climate Change Today and at Home

Where we live, close to the Swiss and French Alps, the glaciers most of the local population depends on for freshwater have evaporated at dramatic rates. In the medium to long term, that could even imperil the water supply of Switzerland's great cities, including Geneva, Zurich, Luzerne, and others, which are all located on the lakes that have been depended on since time immemorial. Or consider Chamonix, France, where Peter has a holiday home. In that area, the famous Mer de Glace or ice sea of the Mont Blanc mountain range—which includes the highest mountain in Western Europe, the Mont Blanc—disappeared so quickly that photos from a few decades ago now almost seem fake. The mountain train station that used to be located right by the glacier is now at the edge of a deep cliff. Instead of walking right on the glacier, visitors must descend 500 steps, and walk hundreds of meters to get a glimpse of the glacier. Mountaineers can no longer climb to the top of the Mont Blanc during several weeks a year because the melting and shifting of the ice has created dangerous crevasses and the risk of avalanches and falling rocks.[20] Those that still risk the crossing during those times, the local mayor warned, have to pay a €15,000 deposit to cover for their possible repatriation and burial services because the death toll on the mountain has risen as climate change accelerated.[21] When a Bloomberg journalist recently visited the premises and learned about these dire consequences of extreme heat driven by climate change, he concluded that "the golden era of European mountaineering is coming to an end."[22]

But harmful exploitation of natural resources goes far beyond hydrocarbons. As briefly mentioned in the beginning of this book, six raw materials—sand, salt, iron, copper, oil, and lithium—form "the fabric of civilization" today, as journalist Ed Conway put it.[d] "Without them, normal life as we know it would disintegrate." That would be fine if our use of these resources diminished over time, or if we learned how to recycle them en masse and ad infinitum. But that is not the case as Conway, who traveled the world to learn more about our exploitation of these resources, found. The holes that are dug and mines that are built to exploit iron, for example, are "mindboggling," according to Conway. The way in which mining companies extract lithium and excessively use water in regions such as Salar de Atacama, Chile, feels to locals like they are "raping Mother Nature." And the vast quantities of rock that are reduced to granules to obtain gold in places like Mount Tenabo, Nevada—a sacred place for the Western Shoshone people indigenous to the region—are "both awe inspiring and disturbing," he wrote.[23]

The most problematic thing about these findings is that they are not anecdotal but part and parcel of our global economic system. If anything, our dependence on these materials is increasing, while the harmful exploitation that is needed to obtain them worsens. Said Conway, "In the countries whence Americans and Britons import most of their goods, [material consumption] is rising at a breakneck speed. Indeed, gold mines in Nevada are the barest fraction of it. We go to far more extraordinary lengths to extract copper and oil, iron and cobalt, manganese and lithium from the ground. . . . Far from being a sideshow, this activity is getting more important, not less . . . in the coming decades we are likely to extract more metals from the earth's surface than ever before."

----

[d] In other parts of the Alps, the melting of the glaciers is endangering the survival of communal life itself. Brienz, a small town in the canton of Graubünden, had to be entirely evacuated in spring 2023 because a rockslide threatened to obliterate the village. The permafrost higher up in the mountains of Brienz had started to thaw, BBC reported, and the rocks inside it started to move down. With heavy rains, the rockslide accelerated, and threatened to destroy the town below. In the end, the rockslide missed the village "by a hair," allowing residents to return. But, as the example shows, the realities of climate change affect life everywhere, even the most prosperous countries in the world.

Needless to say, the same concern can be raised over even more basic elements of life, such as air, water, and soil. Harmful industrial practices still pollute the air in many places around the world, including some of the world's most populous cities. Megapolis cities such as Beijing, Mumbai, Kolkata, Hanoi, Taipei, and Hong Kong were all among the most polluted cities in the world at the time of writing, which meant these cities were unhealthy for their people.[24] According to the WHO, "inadequate management of urban, industrial and agricultural wastewater means the drinking-water of hundreds of millions of people is dangerously contaminated or chemically polluted."[25] (And that is just the drinking water for humans—meaning that it disregards the water that acts as a source of life for animals and fish.) And up to 40% of the world's land is now degraded, the UN warned in 2022,[26] pointing to industrial food production as the single greatest contributor to that worrying trend.

André, who lived for most of his youth near an industrial salt farming site, witnessed some of the harmful effects of natural resource overexploitation firsthand. But he also saw a glimpse of what is possible when business adopts a new nature and works with nature, not against it. Indeed, the salt harvesting in the Rhone Delta, cattle farming in the region, the tourism to Southern France, and the bird sanctuary of the Camargue today *have* found a good form of coexistence. It's this coexistence, in fact, that is depicted in the cover of this book: up top, you can see flamingoes, who spend their summers in the coastal waters of the Camargue. Down below, you can see the salt harvesting, which is sold to consumers under the brand name "Sel de Camargue." Both activities happen side by side, and without imperiling each other. The salt company even welcomes and promotes the presence of the flamingoes on its sites, for the positive effect it has on its image. But if it weren't for the pushback environmentalists did for decades, these kinds of stories might not have ended so well, and indeed they haven't (yet), in most other parts of the world. Even today, harmful exploitation and pollution often win out against less intrusive economic practices. There really is no excuse for it. We're cutting the roots of the tree we live in.

But there is cause for hope, too. The potential for change is just as nearby. Nature's resilience is remarkable, and as soon as humans work with it, not against it, amazing things can happen. Some types of harvesting of renewable energy are among the best examples of that potential, including geothermal energy or wind energy, as we mentioned previously. But the real unsung hero in tackling the climate crisis, says Jean-Pascal Tricoire, the longtime CEO and chairman of Schneider Electric, is energy efficiency.[27] It is the equivalent of leaning less on nature to begin with. (We'll meet Tricoire and his company also in Chapter 8.) With more people on the planet, we don't actually need more energy, or resources, if we are more efficient and regenerative in using them.

Relatively simple techniques such as heat pumps have become amazingly effective in heating people's homes, while leaving a drastically reduced environmental footprint. Schneider Electric estimates, for example, that its new office building in Grenoble, France, located just a few dozen miles from Chamonix and Lake Geneva as the crow flies, uses just a tenth of the energy of its counterparts elsewhere on the continent. That is thanks in great part to "on-site energy storage, and sensors and software that optimize energy-consuming activities such as lighting, heating and cooling"[28]—techniques, in other words, that are available to anyone, anywhere, in the developed world.

In heavy industries and commodities, too, a lot of progress has already been made to be more circular and resource efficient, and is only waiting to be more widely deployed. Glass, for example, can almost infinitely be recycled[29]—although that takes a fair amount of energy—and modern sorting and cleaning techniques have taken away prior barriers to do so. Peter visited one such state-of-the-art glass recycling factory near Bologna, Italy, where glass is sorted, cleaned, and recycled in what the operating company, Sibelco, calls a *closed-loop recycling process*.[30] Theoretically, the same is true for many metals, including steel. And even cement, one of the hardest-to-abate commodities in terms of CO_2 emissions, is proving to be more recyclable than was previously thought possible (you can read more about this in Chapter 7). Working with nature, not against it, means relying much more on these kinds of circular technologies, which put an end or at least a limit to waste, emissions, and extraction. Again, there is no excuse not to pursue these wholeheartedly.

Going a step further, techniques that are explicitly nature-based are surfacing as well. It helps tackle the climate crisis we are facing, but it would also create an economic and social system more in balance with nature, yielding all kinds of additional benefits to humanity's life on earth. The planet is a complex system, which cannot be optimized by looking at one, artificial dimension. Understanding nature as a complex system, and working with it, is thus a much better recipe for success—including economic success—than focusing *exclusively* on extracting resources to make money. The latter is bound to lead to harmful real-life externalities, which society and the economy will end up paying for sooner or later.

This more harmonious approach is already experimented with, including as a business model. In areas affected by storms and other extreme ocean weather, for example, reintroducing mangroves is proving key in protecting human populations living in nearby cities—and lowering their risk of economic losses caused by extreme weather. Indeed mangroves act as a natural barrier against floodings and other natural hazards, reducing the potential damage done by extreme weather. For this reason, insurers such as Axa have started to investigate mangrove protection to make these regions more insurable again. In Vietnam, for example, Axa estimated that investing in mangroves in the Mekong and Red River Delta could reduce the cost of wind damage in the country by half and earn back its investment of $250 million nine times in terms of the damage avoided. In the US and the Caribbean, Axa and the University of California identified 3,000 km of coastline across 20 states, territories, and countries where "post-storm mangrove restoration, which could be paid for by insurance and other mechanisms, would provide flood protection benefits that significantly outweigh the cost of mangrove rehabilitation."[31]

It must be said, though, that Axa's plans have not yet materialized. The reason is that the economic incentives of who invests and who gains aren't aligned. That must rapidly change. "Climate change is already making parts of America uninsurable,"[32] Vox reported in 2023, and *The Economist* said some 45 million people in the US have either already seen increased rates due to increased fires, floods, or wind, or face climate risks yet to be reflected in their premiums.[33] In 2024, the *Financial Times* said we're headed for an "uninsurable world" because of climate change and called rising premiums a "de facto 'carbon price.'"[34]

One company that has been successful at creating the first revenue streams from mangrove restoration is Replanet[e] (Andre's daughter Isabel is on the board of Replanet, and one of the company's instigators.) The company restores and conserves mangroves, but also native forests and marine ecosystems.[35] It monetizes these projects by generating "carbon credits" and "biodiversity credits." Companies that have either committed to decarbonization or biodiversity targets can buy the "credits" generated by Replanet and claim them as their own, either to offset the climate impacts of their business activities or as part of their environmental, social, and governance commitments. Replanet already has a initiated a mangrove project in Central America and has dozens more projects in the pipeline across multiple ecosystems in more than 15 countries.

The practice of reforestation and afforestation (introducing forests in new areas) could also turn out be an effective way to restore climate and nature, though it has its own caveats. Trees are one of the best and most durable ways to capture carbon because they can stand for centuries, while taking in carbon in a matter of years or decades. (They even continue to store significant amounts of

---

[e] Replanet is officially spelled as rePLANET. We use the alternative spelling here to provide consistency with the spelling of other company names.

carbon after they die and decay. Their carbonated remains are what lead to coal and oil millions of years down the line.) Initiatives such as the One Trillion Trees campaign of the World Economic Forum are already banking on this solution and are proving to be one of the least politically divisive and most universally supported nature-based solutions. National chapters exist both in the US and China, for example, as well as in dozens of other countries, showing that "more trees" is one of the few ideas that everyone in the world get behind.[f] The Trillion Tree campaign was also one of the few climate- and nature-related solutions that the Trump administration got behind in its 2017–2021 term,[36] a policy attributed to Ivanka Trump,[37] then a senior advisor to her father, when he was president. Several companies are also turning tree planting and forest management into a business model, selling the "carbon credits" of the forests to companies and governments that use them to offset their carbon emissions.

But the practice of tree planting has growing pains. Tree plantations are often poorly thought through, a *Financial Times* investigation found,[38] providing fewer ecosystem benefits than was expected. The offsets could be tampered with and are at risk of being double or triple counted, or sold but not materialized. And there is the greater issue that carbon credits provide an incentive for companies to continue their exploitative business models, instead of internalizing a nature-based one.

For these reasons and more, we favor planting trees and managing forests, but not as a leading global carbon offsetting or biodiversity credit system—at least not now. There is a danger in over-relying on one variable in our economic system. That is true for short-term profit or share prices, it is true for carbon emissions, and it is true for tree planting.

---

[f] The immediate challenge with this solution, obviously, is how to manage it and account for it. The planting of monocultures, for example, is much less advantageous to nature than a more diversified, natural, and longer-lasting type of reforestation. And the carbon accounting that has come up as an adjacent industry alongside tree planting has experienced the kind of challenges that infant industries often face, including fraud and inaccuracies.

There is more promise in using reforestation and afforestation for a combination of environmental, social, and economic purposes. Good examples of that latter approach are Replanet's method, which looks at the wider ecosystems it operates in, or the rewilding and other greening techniques practiced in cities and on the countryside all over the world. They help mitigate some of the challenges posed by 250 years of industrialization and urbanization.

In Singapore, for example, the greening of the city and its rooftops is an essential element of the city's efforts to keep the hot and humid climate bearable. As a densely populated city close to the equator, Singapore has felt the effects of global warming more than most. Pockets of the city can be up to 6 degrees Celsius hotter than the surrounding countryside, the *New York Times* reported,[39] a reality that will sound familiar to residents of other skyscraper cities from New York to Mumbai. "Almost every aspect of how we build cities amplifies heat, from the buildings we live in to the cars we drive," the *Times* reporters explained, pointing to the omnipresent concrete, the lack of natural airflows, and the exhaust from air-conditioners. But unlike some other cities, Singapore did something about it. It introduced trees and plants everywhere in the city, including the streets and rooftops. It built a 250-acre park in the new Marina Bay neighborhood, rather than fill the expanding city with ever more skyscrapers. And it largely replaced individual A/C units with a centrally managed heating and cooling system. Industrial nature-based solutions are on the rise elsewhere in the world, too, such as the installation of natural water recycling along industrial sites.

The list of these kinds of "nature-based solutions" goes on and on, and they compose of a crucial lever to making our lifestyle as a species more sustainable again, even if they are sometimes still frowned on. We have certainly come a long way since André made his first steps into mainstream business life. Then, in the 1980s, many of the managers and business leaders he encountered shrugged at the notion of nature-based solutions. He was seen as a "tree hugger" for even suggesting these types of solutions.

And if anyone did come up with sustainability projects, it included inconsequential initiatives such as the installation of bird houses near company plants and offices. "That will make him happy," the thinking went.

These days are long gone. As we noted based on Ed Conway's observations previously, companies depend on nature just as much as anyone else. But that is true for consumer-facing companies just as much as it is for mining and raw materials companies. Roche is a good example. The company used plant extracts as the basis of its first medicines back in the late 1800s and early 1900s. Today, Roche and its subsidiary Genentech still use nature, in the form of biological technology, as the basis of their treatments. In fact, nature dependency is just as prevalent in today's economy as it has ever been. Nestlé and other "fast-moving consumer goods" companies depend on nature or the agriculture that stems from it to make virtually anything they sell, including food, water, coffee, and milk, as well. Textile manufacturers such as Nike or Puma rely on cotton and other plants, as well as water, just as much as any weaver did at any point in human history. Construction firms like Holcim need limestone mines and calcine clay to make cement and concrete, and IKEA and other furniture makers need wood to make their furniture. Even artificial intelligence such as Open-AI's ChatGPT would not be possible if it wasn't for the chips and semiconductors made by Nvidia and other manufacturers, which rely on "astronomical" amounts of water and rare earth minerals as inputs.[40]

Yet somehow, when we think of the economy, we still see it is as separate from nature, as if it depended only on human ingenuity and money to produce its outcomes. The exploitation of nature was either ignored as an input factor, or minimized, or even celebrated as a victory of man over nature. André remembers how economists would wave off the arguments of the Club of Rome, back in the 1970s, suggesting that since humanity had overcome food scarcity in the past, for example, it could do so again based on its technological progress. Others said that we needn't worry about "peak oil," as every few years, new reserves of oil and gas would be discovered, or that worries about climate change or mass extinction were overblown, because the planet had survived for all these millions of years. To this day, some believe that humanity has some sort of a "cornucopian" ability to extract more and more natural resources from the ground, by its sheer ingenuity.[41] These considerations were foolish then, and they are inacceptable today.

Luckily, some business leaders today already know better. At IKEA, for example, CEO Jesper Brodin has not only transformed his own company's business model to become much more circular and sustainable, such as the introduction of second-hand store-in-stores, and resource-efficient new product design, he is also one of the leaders of The B Team of global business leaders advocating for a more sustainable approach to business. (You'll learn more about his story in Chapter 9.) At Nestlé, though it is often criticized, there is an increasing awareness across the organization, including with CEO Mark Schneider and chairman Paul Bulcke, that the company needs to map its nature-related dependencies and impacts, and act on them. Its Nespresso subsidiary already became a B Corp,[42] for example, underlining its commitment to sustainable business practices, and other heavily nature-dependent products such as chocolate and coffee are also at the front end of more sustainable business practices, with deforestation-free supply chain goals starting in 2025, and other climate and nature goals from now to 2030 and beyond.[43] And at Holcim, historically one of the world's largest emitters of CO_2, then CEO Jan Jenisch and then Chief Sustainability Officer Magali Anderson made a historic commitment in 2020 to become net-zero in emissions by 2050. Their successors have since validated its journey toward that goal with science-based targets.[44]

These are all signs that business is ready to accept people's dependency on nature, end the overexploitation of it, and understand that it needs to work with nature, not against it.

Having discussed the roots of the new nature of business, let us turn to its trunk and tree in Chapter 6.

Chapter 6

Building with Intent, and Leading by Example

J ust like a tree can grow once its roots are firmly anchored, so business can start to thrive once it roots itself in nature. Indeed, once a company's fundaments are built on working with nature, and not against it, it can live up to its purpose (or redefine it), set targets and deliver against them, and even engage in broader societal leadership. In this chapter, we look at these elements. We name these practices the *trunk* and the *crown* of the new nature of business.

The Trunk: Build with Intent

Reflect on your corporate purpose, set goals that go beyond profits, and measure and disclose all your impacts and dependencies.

It is an overused adage that sums up well the current state of corporate management: "what gets measured, gets managed." There is, however, a major issue with the business truism. For most of the industrial age, and up to the present day, we have mainly pursued and measured financial metrics in business. The centricity of revenue growth and financial profitability in assessing business performance is a logical consequence. But it is also a system that does a disservice to the other "capitals" that matter to our society: human, social, and natural capital. Today, they are simply absent from corporate accounting, and therefore from management, board, and investor analyses. It means that V. F. Ridgway's full insight (he came up with "what gets measured, gets managed") is more poignant than ever: "What gets measured gets managed— even when it's pointless to measure and manage it, and even if it harms the purpose of the organization to do so."[1]

Business leaders today should and can reset this system error. They should build their company with intent. That effort should start with rethinking the purpose of their company, and end with measuring not just financial performance but also environmental, social, and human impacts and dependencies, too, to account for the four capitals we highlighted in Chapter 1. The former is an individual company exercise. The latter is a system-wide challenge.

At Roche, as we have discussed, the purpose of the company is "doing now what patients need next." This purpose statement makes it clear both what Roche is about, and—just as important— what it is not about: the company isn't about the sole pursuit of profits. Making money is both a result of and a prerequisite for delivering on its purpose. But it isn't the purpose itself. Here's how Roche's chairman Severin (Schwan) put it: "Our main contribution to society is improving healthcare, developing better medicines, developing better diagnostic tests. This is what really excites me about Roche: the impact we can make on people's lives. And if we are successful, then we create value for all other stakeholders too—physicians, payers, employees, shareholders, and society at large."[2]

Every company should reflect in a similar way about what its purpose is. The benefits, as Peter's former employer, Bain & Company, found in recent research, are legion. A purpose statement, and its corollaries, a mission and vision statement, explain why a company exists, how it plans to achieve its goals, and what the business will ultimately achieve.[3] A good purpose statement, the consulting firm found, helps guide management's thinking on strategic issues (especially during times of change), inspires employees by providing focus and common goals, and establishes a framework for ethical behavior and employee decision-making.

This is not empty consultant speak. At Roche, the purpose statement helped management and employees in recent years to decide which M&A activities to engage in, how to deal with historical responsibility from waste and pollution, or how to motivate employees to contribute to its long-term sustainability. The purpose statement in that sense acted like a compass, which guides decision-making throughout the company and throughout time.

But if a purpose statement can help in deciding the input of corporate decision-making, it cannot measure its outputs and impacts. Historically, the compass for that assessment has been financial performance and forecasting, as embodied through revenues, costs, and profits. That is a problem because, as we noted previously, not all a company's outputs and impacts are measurable in financial costs, revenues, or profits—at least not today. At Roche, for example, the negative externality caused by the company's pollution in the 1950s to 1980s was never present in corporate financial accounting because the damage did not result in direct financial costs (at least not at the time). Similarly, the benefits the company created when it cleaned its waste site weren't visible in the company's profit-and-loss statement either because they were mostly present in intangible societal goodwill, and private citizens' quality of life, as opposed to company revenues.

Over the years, efforts have been undertaken to do something about this shortcoming, both at Roche and in the business world at large. The effort that probably got the most media and corporate attention was the creation of environmental, social, and governance (ESG) metrics and reports. The ESG approach to reporting a company's nonfinancial performance had its origins in the United Nations but was quickly adopted as a risk assessment tool for investors. If a company had a good ESG track record, the reasoning went, it had fewer risks to its business model. If you pay and treat your workers well, for example, there is a lower risk of strikes or walkouts affecting your bottom line. If you are ahead of the curve on climate emissions, you are less prone to paying for carbon credits or losing business because of environmental requirements. And if you have a strong governance in place, you're less likely to lose top management over scandals, corruption, or mismanagement. As a result of this logic, more and more investors over the past decade started to ask companies for their ESG performance, and a whole ESG investment industry emerged.

Today, ESG reports have become mainstream in listed companies, with some 80% to 90% of Fortune 50 companies using them, Peter found.[4] They have a broad scope: ESG metrics typically include anything from CO_2 emissions to water use, from work safety to pay equality, and from board diversity to CEO pay. But although they are a step forward in helping a company deliver on its broader purpose, they are not a panacea. ESG reports often contain more than 100 metrics, forcing management to "chase more than one rabbit," as Isaac Getz of ESCP Business School puts it. It can lead to a lack of management focus, or worse, strategic ambiguity.[5] And although ESG reports solve for an accounting challenge, they are not in and of themselves a management decision tool. They do not provide a big picture of future scenarios that management can choose from when making an investment decision.

A good example of the benefits and shortcomings of the ESG approach to sustainability comes from Roche itself. From the late 2000s, the company decided it wanted to become a top performer on the Dow Jones Sustainability Index (DJSI), an ESG-inspired list. The index was started by market data firm Dow Jones in 1999 and was intended to give investors a measure of which companies championed "sustainable business practices."[6] Because Roche's own knowledge about sustainability was limited at the time, it believed that working on the DJSI indicators was a "good start," Severin, who was then CEO, told us. On the DJSI, performance was tracked through 20 "financially relevant sustainability criteria" across the ESG spectrum.[7] The governance dimension focused mostly on corporate governance, risk management, and anti-corruption, and the social dimension measured labor practices, talent management, and human capital development indicators. The environmental dimension included measures of CO_2 emissions, the use of natural resources, and waste management.

Roche showed that making ESG scores a focus could yield positive results, not in the least in rankings: the company quickly got recognized as a "sustainability leader" in the DJSI and improved many internal ESG-related processes during this time. It topped the charts in its industry early on and remained among the best-in-class since.[8] Over that same period of time the stock prices never fell below the level it had when the company started to focus on ESG performance, despite going through two mega cycles. Big picture: Roche's stock price went from about 150 CHF in 2010 to about 250 CHF in 2023.[9] A causal link was never proven, but the correlation was there.

In any case, Severin told us, what was once a "good start" is no longer sufficient today. For one, DJSI is no longer the holy grail of sustainability ratings. Dozens of other indices have seen the light of day, and a company's performance on them can differ significantly. "I'm trying to find my way in the jungle of institutions, guidelines, and frameworks," Severin told us. "But there is a proliferation." Logically, then, there is no clarity on which companies are truly sustainable, or what a template looks like. "If you ask: 'who is the most sustainable company?', you have . . . myriad [possible answers]," Severin continued. "Is it Roche in the healthcare industry because we lead DJSI?" That is no one credible response, he believes. And as mentioned, even if there was a single ESG index, it still only would show how a company performs on the indicators it includes over time. It wouldn't help management decide how it could make decisions on the future business models of their company. ESG performance only allows for incremental improvements of an *existing* business model, but it doesn't provide much help in coming up with *novel* business models that may provide a sea change in how a company relates to the world.

Broadly, two possible approaches are needed to address these shortcomings. On the one hand, one could try to translate non-financial measures of sustainability into sole financial value, providing a single measure of transparency and comparability for all a company's impacts and dependencies. On the other hand, companies could create new management accounting tools so they can decide whether to pursue new projects and business models based on both financial and nonfinancial expected impacts.

Note: in what follows you will encounter many organizations, their acronyms, and technical descriptions. We'll do our best to present them in a comprehensible and comprehensive manner but be aware that the proliferation of acronyms and standards in this field has caused many people to conclude there is an "alphabet soup" in sustainability metrics and measures.

Climate- and Nature-Related Financial Disclosures and Targets

An example of the first approach—that of translating sustainability measures into financial measures—is the recently developed set of "climate-related financial disclosures" of the International Sustainability Standard Board (ISSB). (The ISSB is an arm of the IFRS Foundation that has historically set global financial reporting standards, the International Financial Reporting Standards, or IFRS.)

Climate-Related Financial Disclosures and Targets

In 2023, the ISSB released its climate-related disclosure standard, called *IFRS S2*, to standardize how companies disclose material information about their climate-related risks and opportunities to the capital markets. This climate standard, released in conjunction with a sustainability-related financial disclosure standard (IFRS S1), was conceived in such a way as to provide *reliability*, *transparency*, and *comparability* for investors who were trying to understand a company's climate track record—and mostly how it translated into the company's future financial performance.

To make this all a bit clearer, it's worth looking at what the IFRS S2 means in practice. Concretely, the climate standard asks companies to make the following disclosures:[10]

- Disclose your *total* absolute gross greenhouse gas emissions (your *direct* emissions from burning fossil fuels, or from purchasing electricity in-house, and your *indirect* emissions, meaning those of your suppliers and your customers).
- Indicate what amount and percentage of your assets are "vulnerable" to climate-related transition risks, physical risks, and opportunities.
- Disclose what "internal carbon prices" you use to account for the damages and risks posed by greenhouse gas emissions and whether there are remuneration incentives for management that are linked to climate-related considerations and the percentage they represent.
- Describe your greenhouse gas emissions reduction targets and pathway (if any); your climate resilience strategy; and—if applicable—how your "climate scenario analysis" compares with the Paris Agreement, and why.
- Describe the current and anticipated effects of those short-, mid-, and long-term risks and opportunities on the financial statements.

The ISSB's chairman, Emmanuel Faber, told us the ISSB's sustainability disclosures are described in a language directly connected to companies' financial statements, and is ensured by financial auditors. That approach enables creating *market pricing mechanisms* in the way investors allocate capital, he said.

But the climate disclosures of ISSB also fit into a broader effort to come up with a *management decision tool* for climate-related business projects. That effort started in 2015 under the umbrella of the Taskforce on Climate-Related Financial Disclosures (TCFD), which the ISSB Standards incorporate. The TCFD came up with a framework for how companies could set climate-related targets.

In doing so, it helped company management teams to see the bigger picture of various business activities. It helped them answer questions such as, do we align with science-based targets to keep the world within 1.5 degrees Celsius warming? And if not, what kinds of actions and decisions will get us there?

These two activities—setting targets and making disclosures—go hand in hand. The TCFD climate *targets* enable companies to make strategic decisions about their future activities; the *disclosures* enable them to create transparency and trust in their performance toward these targets. In July 2023, the Financial Stability Board of the G20 (a governmental group of the world's largest economies) even declared the publication of IFRS S2 climate standards by ISSB as the "culmination" of the TCFD's work and transferred the TCFD framework to the ISSB.[11]

How the ISSB Disclosures Affect Investor Decisions: A Hypothetical Example

A hypothetical example probably helps understanding the consequences of climate-related financial disclosures such as the ISSB's.

Imagine two car companies, one that is set to only produce electric cars in the future (GreenCo), and one that wants to keep making only gasoline-powered cars (BlackCo). Imagine further that both companies sell the same number of cars, at a similar price, and that until now, neither company has sold any fully electric car. The first, though, is in a transition, and sells only hybrid cars, aiming to fully "electrify" its range by 2035. The other has stuck fully with gasoline cars. In the stock market, you might see minor differences between the two companies, but it's not quite certain that they would be huge (at least not in a market environment where CO_2 disclosures are not mandatory): some investors would appreciate the difference in the future potential of electric vehicles, or of the hybrid vehicles already *on sale, and therefore value GreenCo more. Others, however, might look only at the current sales and profit performance of each company, and the fact that many consumers still plan to buy thermic cars in the future. Such no-nonsense investors may keep the share price of BlackCo high.*

The introduction of the ISSB Standards, however, would have a major impact on the stock market fate of these companies. Suddenly, the information investors receive would be much more meaningful financially. The first disclosure, of current direct and indirect greenhouse gas emissions (required by the ISSB Standards), would show a first difference between the two companies, as the lifetime emissions of GreenCo's hybrid cars are lower. But it's really in the second and third ISSB requirements outlined previously, that a major discrepancy would emerge: for BlackCo, all its financial assets would be "vulnerable" to climate-related risks because it has no plans to phase out gasoline cars (although several major car markets are in fact introducing CO_2 emissions rules). For GreenCo, however, the climate-related risks would be much lower. Not only does it currently produce cleaner cars but also its R&D spent is a climate-related opportunity, rather than a risk. Finally, BlackCo probably doesn't have any pay incentives for management regarding greenhouse gas emissions, nor an internal carbon price. The opposite is likely true for GreenCo.

The consequence of the ISSB Standards, then, is that they would likely push both companies toward net-zero emissions strategies over time. Once investors would see the climate-related differences between companies in an industry, and their at-risk assets, they would be likely to put a premium on those companies that are less risky and have more upward potential and put a discount on those in the opposite situation. The approach followed by ISSB would thus likely accelerate the move toward a decarbonization of the global economy. The ISSB uses existing market mechanisms, and existing financial methods, helping investors see which aspects of a company's climate-related activities are material to them.

Emmanuel Faber and the ISSB's "Investor" Materiality Focus

The ISSB's climate-related financial disclosures are a step in the right direction for anyone who is environmentally minded. But they are particularly a vindication for Emmanuel Faber, the chairman of ISSB, who has spent his life working on the inside to make companies and markets better. (Emmanuel is a friend of André's, and a fellow B Team leader—more on that in Chapter 9.)

As a person, Emmanuel cares about the environment perhaps more than anyone. He's an avid mountaineer and can often be found in the very Mont Blanc mountain range we described previously. He grew up near Grenoble, one of the nearest cities to the French Alps, and has been climbing the Alpine mountains ever since. It gave him a very close up look into the effects of climate change, and a passion to do something about it as a professional. In 2022, he even wrote a book about that double life mission called Ouvrir une Voie, *or* Opening a Route.[12] *He wrote the book in the mountains and presented it in Chamonix to the public.[13]*

But despite this, Emmanuel's road to chairing the ISSB, and presenting its climate-related disclosures, was a rocky one. In 2021, as the COVID crisis was in full swing, Emmanuel wasn't at all working on international accounting standards. He was the CEO of Danone, one of the world's largest consumer good companies, and known in the US from brands such as Dannon and Activia yogurt, Horizon milk, or Evian water. Emmanuel had brought his own passion for sustainability to Danone and merged it with the company's long-standing mission of creating value for itself and its communities. Already in 1972, the company's then CEO, Antoine Riboud, decried the corporate world's single-minded pursuit of profits. "We can't accept that growth would leave behind so many people, especially workers," he said at a speech in France's southern port city of

Marseille. "It is a matter of collective conscience."[14] Four decades later, that mindset, and Danone's "double mission" fit Emmanuel like a glove.

During his tenure as CEO, which started in 2014, Emmanuel wanted to engrain the company's social mission in its bylaws, processes, and business goals. A good way to do so, he believed, was to turn the company into a "benefit corporation." (The legal purpose of a benefit corporation, to use a US definition, is to create a "general public benefit" for its stakeholders, in addition to financial profits for its shareholders.[15]) Over the years, several of Danone's subsidiaries, including the North American one, gained the certified B Corp label, which is based on an outside assessment, and the provision of thousands of ESG data points. In 2017, when Danone USA acquired WhiteWave Foods (known because of Land O'Lakes, Silk, and Alpro, among other brands) in a multibillion-dollar merger,[16] the newly formed entity was incorporated in Delaware as the largest Public Benefit Company in the US.[17] And in 2020, the crowning achievement followed: Danone legally became a "mission-driven enterprise"—the French legal equivalent of a benefit corporation.

But just as Emmanuel reached the zenith of his career at Danone it all came crashing down. In the following year, as COVID put the global economy in a tailspin, an activist investor in Danone pushed for Emmanuel's ouster. Bluebell, the tiny investment firm leading the charge, contended that Emmanuel's leadership was hurting shareholder returns. Since he took the helm in 2014, the earnings had grown by 50%, but the share price of Danone had essentially flatlined because COVID had hurt more of its business categories. At the same time, Danone's key competitors—Nestlé, Unilever, and P&G—had all seen their share price go up. Bluebell's partner, Marco Taricco, told the Financial Times *at the time that "while he supported Faber's strong environmental and social focus, the issue was*

(continued)

(continued)

governance—and financial performance."[18] "*The first duty of a public company is to remunerate shareholders,*" *Taricco said. When Peter spoke to Bluebell's other partner, Giuseppe Bivona, for a* Fortune *article, he echoed that narrow perspective on the role of a company in society—and that they should stay out of politics.*[19] *In any case, the putsch worked. Several other minority investors in Danone piled on to the pressure, and Emmanuel was forced to resign. (Three months later, the company announced that nearly the whole board of directors would be replaced*[20] *for having poorly managed the governance crisis that led to Emmanuel's departure.)*

Seen from that light, the ISSB's sustainability and climate-related disclosure standards, released in 2023, were Emmanuel's second act. They were his opportunity to show the world that having a (nonfinancial) purpose could ultimately deliver financial performance—and that he knew that all along. It helps explain, perhaps, why the ISSB approach has been on what experts call "single materiality," or what Emmanuel calls "investor materiality." The disclosures ISSB asks companies to report on, are namely the ones that can be translated into financial impact on the company. Conversely, they talk about the company's impact on the wider world (what Emmanuel calls impact materiality, *and which is often described as "double" materiality) only to the extent that this might affect the company's prospects and investor decisions. They do not require information about impacts on the world that have no impact on the company and its cost of capital. (In our hypothetical example in the previous box, Emmanuel pointed out, the ISSB's Climate Standard would require the disclosure of direct and indirect emissions along the value chain. It means that if GreenCo and BlackCo disclose the ISSB metrics, their greenhouse impact on the planet and society would be known—because ISSB has established that indirect emissions, too, may be material for investors.)*

Emmanuel is convinced that his focus on "investor" material-ity is the most "immediately powerful" way to put the markets to work in the climate transition today, he told Peter in an interview in 2023—as opposed to a focus on the "double" or "impact" mate-riality. "The word materiality, which comes from the accounting world, is misused," he said. "Double materiality is a false positive. It was a good idea. But when you go into the precision, it becomes much more complex." According to Emmanuel, the better choice, thus, is to focus on investor materiality. As it moves trillions of dollars every day, it will ultimately lead much faster to the same outcome, he believes. "Our theory of change is a better functioning capital market, where investors can allocate capital to what is more useful to them," he told Peter. "Today they [the investors] are blind to risks that underlie the sustainability space. To deal with that, we need to speak the language of decision-making for capital markets. That is where we are. I will not deviate. We will not be true to that mission if we deviate."

Although we see what Emmanuel means, we still support the development of disclosures that allow for both "single" (or "investor") materiality, and "double" (or "impact") materiality calculations. And, crucially, we believe it is necessary that not only climate-related disclo-sures find their way to the corporate world, but nature-related ones, as well. (At the time of writing, the ISSB said it was working on such nature-related disclosures.) In the latter, we believe a double material-ity approach is certainly needed, as a company's nature impacts and dependencies are often much more local and clear-cut.

Nature-Related Financial Disclosures and Targets

A second, nascent example of how sustainability is translated into financial disclosures and targets comes from the Taskforce on Nature-Related Financial Disclosures (or TNFD)—the twin organization to the TCFD. In September 2023, the TNFD released its own recommendations, which went far beyond climate: they included freshwater, oceans, land, and the atmosphere—all "nature's four realms," as the TNFD put it (see Figure 6.1). But if the scope was vastly broader, in many other ways the TNFD did work just like its climate counterpart. Like the TCFD, the TNFD will most likely be a crucial building block for organizations such as the ISSB because they develop nature-related financial disclosures that any company could use, and any investor or stakeholder could understand. And, like the TCFD's, the TNFD recommendations give companies a framework to base their future *decisions* on an understanding of the impact they will have on nature.

Compared to the climate-related disclosures, the nature-related disclosures will be the real milestone in creating the new nature of business, we believe. They will show the full interdependency

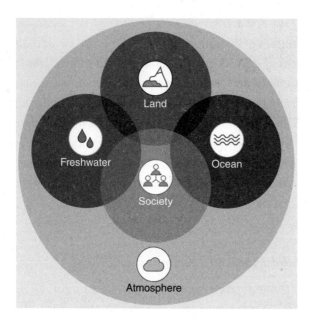

Figure 6.1   Nature's four realms, with society at the center: land, freshwater, ocean, and atmosphere.

Source: TNFD Recommendations, 2023 / TNFD / CC BY 4.0.

among business, nature, and society. If companies manage to include nature-related targets and disclosures throughout their organization, including in strategy, risk management, and accounting, the economic system we live in will look entirely different from the one we have today. But we are not yet there, for at least three reasons.

First, nature-related disclosures and targets are more complex than climate-related ones. The climate-related financial targets and disclosures, as we saw, can be applied by companies today, thanks to the existence of science-based targets for climate, and climate-related financial disclosures. Regulators can start to adopt the ISSB's climate-related sustainability standards in their accounting rules, and companies can start reporting on them. The nature-related financial targets and disclosures, however, are still in their infancy. It won't be until 2026 that the first companies will pioneer the use of this framework, and the disclosures that come with it, in their annual reports. And it will take at least another few years until organizations such as the Science Based Targets Network, which as the name suggests helps companies set science-based targets, and the ISSB, which develops disclosures, will have turned them into international standards that any company can use.

There is a second reason nature-related disclosures will take a longer time to implement. For nature-related disclosures, much more than for climate-related ones, a so-called double materiality approach seems warranted. (As a quick reminder, "single materiality" means that you look only at how a sustainability-related factor, such as climate change, affects business, and you do not look at how an individual business affects that same factor. "Double materiality" means that you measure and report on both relationships. For a visual explanation, see Figure 6.2.)

In the case of climate, as we explained in a separate text box, you can make the argument for "single materiality" (or "investor materiality" as Emmanuel Faber calls it). But the situation is different for nature-related impacts and dependencies. The relation between business and nature is often more local than that between

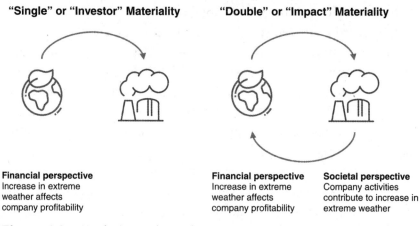

Figure 6.2　Single (or traditional) materiality versus double materiality.

Source: palau83/Adobe Stock and lushik/DigitalVision Vectors/Getty Images.

business and climate. The good news is that this opens the door to a "double materiality" (or "impact materiality") assessment because companies can observe and measure their nature-related impacts at that local level. But the bad news is that measuring this impact materiality comes with its own new and unique challenges: it involves a lot of (local) stakeholders, which are each affected in their own way, and it requires bringing all impacts back to a single measuring unit. (Not to mention how these interacting impacts and dependencies should be governed.) Thus, although a double materiality approach is warranted, it also creates new problems. The most wicked among them is that, for accounting purposes, the impact on nature at this point does not have one "language." Let's look at an example to make it concrete.

For Danone, to take the example of the company Emmanuel Faber used to lead, selling Evian water is obviously dependent on having access to . . . Evian water. It has been a profitable business for a very long time, but also an extremely nature-dependent one.[21] Since the 1800s, Evian water has been bottled and sold by a private company—the "Société anonyme des eaux minerales d'Evian."[22] Today, Evian is a blockbuster brand, with an annual output capacity of 2 billion bottles,[23] and billions of dollars in retail sales.) The financial revenue Danone generates with its Evian plant is thus just one of the dimensions of this business. From a nature perspective, Evian *depends on* the water in the surrounding French Alps. But the bottler's presence in the lakeside town also *affects the availability of* water for other purposes, such as municipal water supply. And by exporting its water and selling it in plastic bottles all around the world, Evian also creates nature-related impacts beyond its source of origin. The nature-related financial disclosures the TNFD and others are working on, would optimally enable Danone or other stakeholders to reveal that system of dependencies, risks, opportunities, and impacts in a much clearer way than is possible today—and translate them into economic costs. But that is not a reality today.

The third reason we don't yet see nature related disclosures in corporate management is that some of a company's impacts on nature are more "silent and invisible" than its climate-related impacts. Climate change is the most urgent problem we face. We've been able to bring it back to a single cause we can focus on—greenhouse gas emissions. We are increasingly able to "price" it as an externality. At least in theory, that provides companies with an adequate mechanism to do something about them. Climate change in that way is a bit like the hole in the ozone layer, or acid rain caused by pollution. In the 20th century, society and business were able to address these problems because it was so clear what caused them and what would solve the problem.

For nature, the situation is different. Some effects of current business practices won't be known about for decades, or even centuries to come. Other effects are becoming apparent, but we won't know just how bad they will affect us. Plastic pollution of the oceans, for example, may have vast and long-lasting consequences for life in the oceans—and on earth. But what we can do about it, once plastic has degraded into microplastics, and has entered living organisms, is much less certain.

Using up natural resources that the earth has taken millions of years to create may hurt generations hundreds, thousands, or millions of years down the line. But we don't know for sure, and cannot properly price it today because most resources are still abundantly available. The waste we create now, and the destruction we bring about, may also bring about permanent damage. But we cannot price them in the same way as we can price carbon emissions, because many waste and destruction zones are far removed from the cities most of us live in.

For all these reasons, it will be more complicated for companies to fully include nature-related financial disclosures throughout their organization. It is time we don't have. In the interim, it is necessary that business takes another step when it comes to its interaction with nature: set nonfinancial targets as business.

How UN Goals and Corporate Targets and Disclosures Fit Together

Including UN goals into the management of a company may seem disjointed at first. But there is a logic to the madness. It goes as follows:

- *In a first phase, an international agreement is made between governments, on a global challenge like climate change or biodiversity loss. That usually happens at the UN Conference of the Parties. Notably,*
  - *In 2015, there was such an agreement on climate at the UN climate change convention in Paris. It said the world wanted "to limit the temperature increase to 1.5°C above pre-industrial levels,"[24] and led to a target of achieving net-zero CO_2 emissions by 2050.[25]*
  - *In 2022, there was a similar agreement at the Convention on Biodiversity meeting in Montreal/Kunming on biodiversity. Its goals included protecting 30% of the earth's land and water by 2030, restoring another 30% of degraded lands and waters.[26]*

- *Following this agreement, national governments, and international institutions such as the European Union decide on their "national contributions." They may also set additional rules and regulations that apply to all companies operating in their country or region.*
- *In a second phase, groups like the Science Based Targets initiative (SBTi), and the Science Based Targets Network (SBTN) may help companies translate these global and national goals into targets that specifically apply to them. For example,*
  - *Holcim, a construction materials company we will meet in Chapter 7, worked with SBTi to set specific targets on its CO_2 emissions for its net-zero journey, from 2021 on all the way until 2050. This is important, because Holcim is historically responsible for up to 0.5% of all global CO_2 emissions.*
  - *GSK, the pharmaceutical firm, worked with the SBTN in 2023 on setting targets for its freshwater use.[27] In a later phase, they will also work on targets for how they affect oceans, land areas, and so on.*
- *Concurrently, taskforces like the TCFD and the TNFD work on general recommendations on climate- and nature-related financial disclosures that all companies can make, regardless of their specific targets. These disclosures concern governance, strategy, risk and impact management, as well as disclosures on CO_2 emissions or the use of natural resources*
- *In a last phase, international standard setters such as ISSB work on standards that all companies around the world can use in their financial reports on climate and nature. Notably, the ISSB released its sustainability standards on CO_2 emissions disclosures, in 2023, as we discussed previously. In a perfect world, these standards are adopted by national regulators all over the world and become part of the mandatory disclosures any company makes in their annual reports.*

The MAVA Foundation for Nature, and Its Link to the Business and Nature Agenda

At this point in the chapter, you may wonder how the climate- and nature-related financial targets and disclosures came about. The answer is it took many years, many partner organizations, and many conversations to come to the fundamental understanding that business and nature truly need to be symbiotic if we want humanity to thrive. It took even longer to establish the right frameworks and targets to do so. But I would be remiss if I didn't mention the role our family's MAVA Foundation played in this process. The MAVA Foundation for Nature,[28] originally conceived by my father in 1994, brought together many pieces of the corporate nature and climate puzzle over the years. It played a foundational role, for example, in the creation of the ISSB and its disclosures, and the TNFD and its implementation/decision-making framework.

It wasn't always meant to be that way. The goal of MAVA when it was created was the conservation of iconic species, such as the great white pelican or the flamingo, in iconic places, such as the Camargue or the Bijagos archipelago in Guinea-Bissau. It was conservation as it used to be done, you could say: a philanthropic organization supporting specific aims.

MAVA's action radius gradually changed in the late 2010s. Until then we were dealing more with the symptoms of human impact on nature, rather than addressing the root causes for it. Once we realized there was this missing link, we (MAVA) started seeking partners who could help us put together a "theory of change" in the world of finance. MAVA also put together a sustainable economy division. It gave small grants at first, and then we did more. In all, MAVA supported hundreds of organizations and individuals working on the sustainable economy.[29]

Before TNFD got up and running, for example, we already sup-ported the creation of a few other initiatives, such as Nature Finance (previously known as the Finance for Biodiversity Initiative).[30] *And when TNFD was ultimately created, we provided seed funding for that organization, too. As for the ISSB, my fellow B Team members and I got together at the COP26 meeting in Glasgow and encour-aged Emmanuel, a fellow B Team member, to take on the chairman-ship of ISSB.*

I mention this history, not to blow the horn of MAVA but as reminder that systems change doesn't occur overnight, and it doesn't happen without people and organizations taking concrete steps toward it. Today, organizations like the ISSB and the TNFD have an increasingly important impact on the world of business. But that might not have been the case, if it wasn't for the preparatory work and funding of organizations such as MAVA.

Going forward, we need much more still of such grassroots work, cross-sectoral collaboration, and seed funding to ensure the business and nature agenda gets even higher on the list of global priorities.

This box is written in André's voice.

Nonfinancial Targets

Given the limitations of nature-related financial disclosures thus far, an alternative for businesses today is to set a small set of non-financial targets, alongside financial ones. At Roche, for exam-ple, management defined a collection of 10-year ambitions to be achieved by the end of the 2020s that were mostly nonfinancial. It stands out, that they address Roche's (contributions to) social, human, and natural capital:

- To improve patient outcomes by delivering transformative med-icines, diagnostics, and digital solutions that address diseases with the highest societal burden

- To create an inclusive work environment through a diverse leadership that truly mirrors the company's workforce
- To reduce the company's environmental impact by half

Only one 10-year ambition addressed the company's financial capital. It is based on improving Roche's *financial enterprise value*.

We feel that this is the right way to go about leading a business:

- Put most of your focus on delivering on your purpose to society.
- Do so while respecting and optimizing human capital, and your environmental impacts and dependencies.
- And as a result, you will (and should) do well financially

In a system driven only by short-term financial considerations, it would be difficult—if not impossible—to simultaneously deliver on the financial *and* the nonfinancial goals. But if you take a longer-term perspective, you also account for the interdependencies with nature, society, and business. In that context, the nonfinancial goals make a lot more sense. In the long run, Roche can only do well in a society and on a planet that do well. So, it should be pursuing medicines addressing diseases with the highest societal burden. And it should reduce its environmental impact. Neither of those stand in the way of generating more revenues and earnings. In fact, contributing to the health of the planet and society is a necessary condition for Roche to do well financially in the long run, not just a moral obligation.

The same logic applies for any company. In the case of Roche, the nonfinancial ambitions are shared by management and shareholders. But increasingly, companies can also rely on outside organizations to help them set targets that make sense in the context of the United Nations Sustainable Developments Goals, the UN Paris Agreement on climate, or the UN Kunming-Montreal Global Diversity Framework. A group of 17 pioneering companies, for example, in 2023 started working with the Science Based Targets Network on initial nature-based targets. In a first instance, they are focusing on freshwater use, but in a later phase, targets on land use and oceans will become available too. Similarly, companies can work with organizations such as EDGE and the World Benchmarking Alliance, which work on gender equity, human rights, digital inclusion, and other targets.

The Crown: Lead and Let Lead

Let 1,000 branches grow. Empower fellow leaders to step forward, recognize the value of democracy and society, and keep a moral compass.

The final aspect of the new nature of business is to lead and let lead. It is about the recognition that a company, like a society, is made up of many people, and that they all have a role to play. Who among them can put in place the new nature of business and society? Who can challenge, be bold, and keep interest of humanity at heart? We need many such leaders.

Roche alone is made up of 100,000 people. For it to be successful in its pursuit of "doing now what patients need next," having the right management committee and top-down targets doesn't suffice. Managers such as Richeal or David, whom we met in Chapter 4, also need to be able to step forward and feel empowered to lead where they can.

The corollary of this kind of decentralized and multipronged leadership is that top management shouldn't expect its colleagues to spend all their time reporting to them. Team members should be able to spend their time on solving problems or representing the company to outside stakeholders. What matters more in the relationship between management and their teams is an agreement on goals and an alignment on shared values and key principles on how people work together. At Roche, those fundamental values are *integrity, courage,* and *passion.* Those are supplemented by operating principles (see Figure 6.3). They go

❶ **Put patients first**	I always act as if patients I know are in the room and do what's best for them.	
❷ **Follow the science**	I seek answers through experiments, data and debate, and act on facts.	
❸ **Act as one team**	I care, collaborate and commit without boundaries, and trust others to do their part.	
❹ **Embrace differences**	I seek diverse perspectives, invite opposing views, and challenge myself and others.	
❺ **Accelerate learning**	I push to learn new things even if difficult, and openly share my successes and failures.	
❻ **Simplify radically**	I eliminate complexity, reuse with pride, and accomplish more with less.	
❼ **Make impact now**	I take accountability to do what's right, deliver value fast, and don't wait for certainty.	
❽ **Think long term**	I choose actions today that benefit future generations.	

Figure 6.3   Roche operating principles.

Source: Roche.

a lot further in guiding people's behavior, than a long list of detailed rules.

The same is true in society at large. For us to create a new economic system, and a new social contract to go along with it, many leaders need to step up, in all layers of society. In this chapter, we have seen that many organizations play a role in this journey: from the UN and its specialized agencies, to international standard setters, and organizations such as the ISSB and the TNFD, to national and local governments and activists. All these organizations and their leaders interact with and depend on each other. In many cases, the events that have a significant effect on a company are not necessarily those that are decided internally in a management committee, but those that come from outside, like a change in regulation or sometimes even a journalistic article or an award.

Equally, a single company cannot create system-wide change. That requires a coalition of companies, with common standards or targets that everyone contributes to.

Most of all, we need good leaders in government, in our communities, and in society at large. Being a leader doesn't always mean taking on a public office, though there is a desperate need for more talented public leaders. In countries like Switzerland, or US states like California, democratic leadership can also mean taking part in a debate on a referendum, for example, or supporting individuals and organizations that do. André did that, for example, when the Swiss people had to vote on the climate referendum in June 2023. He wrote an opinion article in a local newspaper to convince his fellow citizens to support the new climate law,[31] even if it would hurt him financially in the short run just as much as anyone else. (The law was adopted in the referendum.)

These contributions to democracy by business leaders, entrepreneurs, and wealthy individuals should not flow over into a capture by business of democracy, however. As a business leader, you have the right, and perhaps the duty, to speak up on the topics you believe matter to the prosperity and well-being of society. There is a need, too, for consultations between governments and companies on the issues that lie at the intersection of business and society.

But business leaders, entrepreneurs, and other wealthy individuals should make sure they do not advocate only for their narrow self-interest in these interactions, and instead keep the broader societal interests at heart. A good question any leader should ask themselves before taking a public stance or engaging with government on a societal issue is, cui bono? Who benefits from my position? If the only clear beneficiary is you or your company, you may want to rethink your position and take a more enlightened stance. Businesses and their leaders benefit from democratic societies in many ways. In turn, they have a responsibility to support democracy, or at least do no harm to it.

★ ★ ★

In the next chapters, we'll highlight the stories of some companies, organizations, and their leaders who have taken a more holistic view on their role in society. They exemplify the new nature of business. We hope they may serve as an inspiration to those who seek to build such companies and organizations in the years to come or want to contribute to them in their own unique way.

Chapter 7

How the Waste Guy Became a Superhero

"I love concrete." It's a phrase you won't hear very often in real life. But at Holcim, a Swiss multinational construction materials company, it's a credo all employees live by. We noticed it for the first time when we went to visit Holcim's global innovation center in Lyon, France. A company executive proudly repeated the phrase throughout his presentation to a group of journalists. It sounded like an oddity at first, a quirky catchphrase from a man on a PR mission.

But then we started hearing echoes of the same sentiment again and again. We heard it when Magali Anderson, Holcim's first chief sustainability officer until 2023, talked to us about the role of cement and concrete in the world's CO_2 emissions. "We need to get to net-zero concrete production," she said firmly. "But it

---

An earlier, shorter, and edited version of this chapter, authored by Peter, appeared as an advance publication for the December 2023/January 2024 issue of *Fortune Magazine* with the headline, "Concrete Results." "The Construction Industry Has Been a Major Climate Change Offender. This Swiss Company's Cement and Concrete Could Help Builders Get Greener," https:// fortune.com/europe/2023/11/08/climate-change-concrete-cement-holcim-fortune-500-europe/.

would be foolish to throw the baby out with the bathwater, and stop building with concrete," she also insisted. "From a systemic perspective, you need concrete," she said. We even got e-mails, and LinkedIn posts and messages, of people proudly announcing that they, too, loved concrete.

But what is it about the material that has so many people excited about it, especially when it is also responsible for so many CO_2 emissions—at least 8% of global emissions come from the cement industry[1]? More important, could this gray commodity ever play the role of climate and nature hero? To find the answers to these questions, we would love to tell you the story of two concrete-loving individuals. From their offices in Zurich, over the period of a decade, they helped herald a new era for the built environment, based on nature, metrics, and leadership.

★ ★ ★

At first sight, Cathleen Hoffmann (no relation to André) and Clemens Woegerbauer are regular corporate managers, working on run-of-the-mill tasks. Heading up the commercial and product development teams of Holcim Switzerland, respectively, Cathleen and Clemens have been developing concrete products and selling them in the Swiss market for many years. It's a job they are passionate about, just like many people in the construction business. But beyond their direct colleagues and clients, very few people would know of these professionals and their work. The concrete they sell dominates the skylines of Zurich and other Swiss cities. But it's the concrete that is a head turner, not the people behind it.

But in our story, Cathleen and Clemens take center stage. It all started with a client request from Zurich about a decade ago. Eberhard, a local construction firm, approached Holcim with a seemingly innocuous question: could Holcim help Eberhard get rid of its construction waste in Switzerland?

Until then, Eberhard had engaged in expensive landfilling. The company had been eager to avoid the fees for a long time because they added to the firm's costs of doing business without adding any value. But until the firm approached Holcim, it had no viable alternative. The case soon landed on Clemens's desk. At the time, he was known internally as "the waste guy," as his job then consisted of helping Holcim's clients with recycling. And he was happy to look in to the matter. "We like to offer new recycling pathways for materials," Woegerbauer told us in an interview. And there was a good business rationale, too, he said. "At Holcim, we also offer recycling services for a fee." If Holcim could take in Eberhard's waste instead of sending it to a landfill, it would collect the money that would otherwise go elsewhere. The only question was: what would Holcim then do with the waste?

Clemens discussed the matter with another department: that of Cathleen, who worked on product development. The basic premise they started off with was straightforward: if they could turn the waste back into usable construction material, they would gain twice financially: once when collecting the construction waste from Eberhard and once when they sold the recycled product back to Eberhard or other clients. So far, very attractive. And the project could help turn their business into a circular one: instead of mining virgin limestone for every new construction project, they could instead use a recycled form of concrete, a holy grail in terms of sustainability.

It was inconceivable in some ways, but straightforward in others. In fact, a similar approach had been used by Europeans for millennia. From at least Roman times, bricks and stones used in prior buildings were reused to construct new ones. (Peter has a personal history with this technique: his family in Belgium used to own lands on which the remains of an 8th-century church were found,[2] built with recycled stones from an ancient Roman villa. The "recycled" church stood for almost 1,000 years. Similar buildings still stand all over the continent today.)

But the question Clemens, Cathleen, and their colleagues faced was also intractable. By the end of the 20th century, building codes all but prohibited the reuse or recycling of demolition

waste all over Europe—as well as in Holcim's other global markets, including the United States, its largest market with more
than $10 billion in yearly revenues. There was good reason for
these strict rules: some low-quality construction materials used
between the 1950s and 1990s in the UK and other European
countries had turned out to have a lifespan of just 30 years,[3] for
example, leading to a ban on their use. Even the recycling of
stronger concrete, several researchers believed until recently,[4] did
not have the same strength as its "virgin" equivalent, making it a
hazardous affair. If Holcim went by the current laws and regulations, it could simply not help Eberhard.

Or could it? By the early 2000s, landlocked Switzerland had
regulators that were more amenable than most to material recycling, provided structural safety could be proven. The Alpine country's population largely lived on a sliver of land dubbed the *middle
country*, sandwiched in between the Alps and the Jura mountains.
Switzerland's great cities, lakes, agriculture, and industry all had to
share this plateau and make it work for all. The last thing anyone
needed was for this precious land to be used for construction waste
sites, or to mine more of its natural resources than necessary. Since
at least the 2000s, the practice of recycling of construction and
demolition waste had been well established in Switzerland.[5] Going
forward, its regulators were amenable to having a conversation on
how to extend that track record as well.

So, the Holcim team went to work. The immediate business
rationale was enough of an incentive to get the project underway. But just as important was that recycled cement would also fit
into Holcim's long-term business model. The world's built environment of houses and buildings has historically been the single
largest source of CO_2 emissions globally. Still today, it stands at a
staggering 39% of annual emissions.[6] Cement production alone
is responsible for almost a quarter of those emissions because of
the fossil fuels typically used in its production and the chemical
processes that go along with it. Most of the other CO_2 emissions
from the built environment come from the heating and cooling

of buildings. Yet even these emissions ultimately come down to building because building materials with better isolation properties could eliminate the need for much of this heating and cooling.

As one of the largest construction material companies in the world, Holcim is responsible for many of the world's historic and current greenhouse gas emissions. (According to one study commissioned by a party that subsequently sued Holcim, the company was responsible for almost half a percent of the global greenhouse gas emissions from 1950 to 2021.[7]) And, of course, there is a major nature element to the equation as well. Cement and concrete are made primarily of clinker, which in turn comes largely from processed limestone. In the product life cycle today, limestone is first excavated in quarries all over the world. It is then processed so it can be used as a basis for cement and concrete production. And once the concrete buildings have run their course, the demolished concrete ends up in waste fills scattered all over the planet. It leaves the planet at worst with three affected places: the quarries, which often end up looking like scarred mountains; the urban center, of course, where people live; and the waste sites, which turn natural sites into wasteland.

If the Swiss Holcim team could square the circle of construction demolition material recycling, they could help their company go from villain to hero on climate and nature.

★ ★ ★

As Clemens and Cathleen went about their challenge, change was afoot at Holcim's global headquarters as well. In 2017, Jan Jenisch, a manager who had previously led the Swiss chemical firm Sika, was appointed as the company's new CEO. (He has since become chairman.) As an outsider at the then 105-year-old company, Jenisch realized Holcim needed to change to remain relevant in the 21st century. Ever since its founding in the petite Swiss town of Holderbank in 1912—Holcim is short for _Holderbank Ciment_—the company had been expanding through mergers and volume plays. Cement is a commodity, so being the biggest, for a long time, was best.

But as Jenisch took over, the strategy of never-ending mergers and volume plays had to end. For one, after Holcim had merged with its longtime rival, the French Lafarge company, in 2015, there was barely any acquisition target left. And, as the 20th century had given way to the 21st, neither governments nor public opinion were all too keen anymore on the huge amounts of CO_2 the cement industry emitted each year. As we have seen, some governments, such as Switzerland, were worried about the industry's imprint on nature as well. It all pointed to a logical but painful conclusion: for everything in Holcim's world to remain the same, everything had to change.

"When I joined . . . I found strong, locally embedded businesses, 2,300 production sites, right-in-time supply, . . . the largest building material company in the world," Jan told us as he looked back at those early years. But what got Holcim to 2017 wouldn't get it to 2027 or beyond, he also realized. "You have to think about how markets will develop in the future," he said. Those developments still included growth, he firmly believed, given the world's growing population and urbanization. But it would have to be built on different foundations than before: those of innovation and sustainability, rather than commodities and volume. Any other approach would not have societal buy-in.

Jan brought on board a few newcomers to realize his mission. There was Miljan Gutovic, a former colleague at Sika. The Australian was put in charge of Middle East and Africa, and soon afterwards became head of Europe and took charge of the company's decarbonization drive. When we met him in Lyon in summer 2023, he proudly relayed all of Holcim's innovative practices regarding sustainability back to revenues for the firm. (In May 2024 Miljan succeeded Jan as CEO.) And there was Magali Anderson, a French engineer who had spent most of her career working as a "Jill of all trades" at SLB (previously Schlumberger) in the oil industry. At SLB, she had run through roles such as general manager in Angola, global manufacturing manager, and vice president of marketing and sales. At Holcim, she joined as head of safety even before Jan's arrival. Two years into his tenure, she took an even more consequential role: that as first ever chief sustainability officer (CSO).

Before Magali accepted the CSO role, she told us, she advised Jan that Holcim had to be serious about changing its ways. She had joined Holcim in health and safety as she was approaching 50 "to have a bit more purpose in life" and wanting "to wake up in the morning and know that my job was to save people's lives." If she was going to take on the sustainability challenge next, she told Jan, it should be to help save the planet. "If I make Holcim look good, it is a collateral effect," she told him. "If you don't agree with that, don't give me the job." Jan agreed, and gave Magali a free pass, which she carried over into her sustainability assignment.

As chief sustainability officer, Magali was given a seat in the executive committee, and the challenge to keep Holcim relevant in a world marked by two opposing trends: global demographic growth and urbanization on the one hand and the need to operate within planetary boundaries on the other hand, which put obvious strains on the company.

Faced with those two mega-trends, Holcim reimagined its mission. Instead of aiming to sell ever more amorphous cement, Holcim started to see its primarily role as that of "decarbonizing building"[8] and acting as a steward of nature. To an outsider, it may have looked like greenwashing—akin to a cigarette company stating it wants people to stop smoking. And indeed, activist groups such as Renovate Switzerland were and remain wary about Holcim's turn. How could a company that in their view had historically caused so much destruction to climate and nature truly become one of its champions, they wondered. But the new strategy did come with a cold business rationale and a series of targets and metrics.

Magali Anderson, the company's no-nonsense sustainability executive, charged ahead on the targets and metrics front, starting with Holcim's carbon emissions. Rather than setting unrealistic goals far into the future, she enlisted the help of the Science Based Targets initiative we mentioned previously.[9] "I didn't want to be accused of anything," she told us about that outreach. "I wanted to make sure that everything we do is based on science and have a third party validate it." The first science-based goal the company set, in 2019, was for its carbon emissions to be in line with a maximum 2 degrees Celsius global warming. But every year since, Magali turned the screws a little tighter. In 2020, the company recommitted to a science-based goal, but this time for "well below 2 degrees" warming. In 2021, it upgraded to a net-zero carbon emissions goal by 2050. And in 2022, the summum of science-based goals was adopted: one where Holcim would do its part to keep global warming limited to 1.5 degrees Celsius. It put Holcim in line with the most ambitious targets experts believe are possible on a global scale and made it stand out among its peers.

The consequence of committing to those targets was that Holcim needed to decarbonize its operations, and fast. The one advantage it had was that it didn't have to start from scratch. The cement industry overall had been measuring its CO_2 footprint since the 1990s, Magali told us, putting it ahead of almost every other sector in terms of their awareness. And given the scrutiny the company had been getting for its role in climate change, it had already decreased the CO_2 intensity of its cement production by 30% since 1990. Having its global plants adopt best practices of efficiency in production from around the world constituted the low-hanging fruit. But now came the hard part. The company wanted to keep growing its global revenues, just as it got to the "hard to abate" part of its emissions.

Magali and her team set targets, made action plans, and embedded their solutions into the business model of the company. Two of them were rather straightforward. The first was to replace the fuel that fired up the kiln in which cement is made. Traditionally, fossil fuel was used for this purpose, but the company had found that burning wood or certain types of waste were viable alternatives, too. The fuel change alone could reduce CO_2 emissions by up to

30%, Magali said. The second lever was to replace the limestone that went into cement with another, less CO_2-intensive input, such as clay. On a visit to one of their cement plants, in the town of Eclépens, not too far from André's home, Peter saw both techniques at work. A live video feed of the kiln showed how shredded old tires and biomass got burnt into the fire. And calcined clay was used to the extent possible instead of the limestone-based clinker.

A third, more controversial lever, is still under development when you read this book: that of carbon capture, use, and storage.[10] It is a controversial one, Magali realizes, as it implies that carbon *is* still produced in industrial processes. But what makes it a viable option in combatting climate change is that it is consequentially captured, used, and stored so as not to pollute the atmosphere and cause global warming. Magali believes it is a crucial lever because the very chemical nature of cement production means there will always be carbon production.

In its construction projects, too, Holcim aimed to "build better with less." Similar to Roman times, it would experiment with gravitational forces (and metal clamps), rather than mortar, to hold arch-like structures together. That would generate a saving in cement use. In its floorings, it would use concrete only where it had structural effects, and replace it with lighter, less CO_2-heavy product mixes when possible. To make up for the loss in the volume of cement or concrete sold, it came up with new applications for its products, such as 3D printing of buildings, increasing its market in that way. These new applications would still help the company in its decarbonization journey because they enable a more efficient use of cement and concrete versus the traditional way of building.

Finally, Holcim would take a more holistic approach to its role in the building sector. What if its concrete wall and floors could help buildings be carbon-neutral once they are used? And what if its concrete could fit into green urban architecture, rather than to be a nemesis of it? In its revamped global innovation hub in Lyon, France, a team of engineers came up with all kinds of product innovations. On a visit in late summer 2023, Peter saw what those efforts had led to, over a few short years: a superlight isolation layer for roofs, for example, that felt more like chocolate mousse than concrete and could be used as isolation material both in hot and cold climates. Or concrete walls with plant seeds mixed in, which then turned the walls into Babylonesque-like hanging gardens over time, as rain poured through them.

Some of those innovations are still more like what concept cars are for car manufacturers: proof of the company's imagination and engineering prowess. Others have turned into products that have real-world impact already today.[a] A recently finished school in Vienna, Austria, is an excellent case in point. Finished in early 2023, the Vienna school, entirely built with state-of-the-art Holcim products, can cover 90% of its energy needs through internal geothermal processes, the school found.[11] It means that whether in summer or in winter, the school doesn't need much gas or electricity to operate. Heat pumps, solar roof panels, isolation, and other techniques take care of most of the use needs of the building. (The concrete in the building is designed for thermal activation to serve as a battery, storing or releasing heat to meet the building's needs, the company pointed out to us.) It is proof of how human ingenuity can solve the greatest of planetary challenges, as long as companies put their mind to it.

★ ★ ★

Back in Holcim's Swiss offices, Clemens's and Cathleen's teams were progressing on their solution for Eberhard. The product development team, for starters, had identified a way to reuse construction waste and make a reliable new type of cement and concrete with it. The process included crushing the old material, cleaning it of any impurities, and then mixing it in with virgin

---

[a] The company noted that 90% of its patent applications since 2021 support its sustainability targets, that it brought 600 new products to the market in 2023 alone, and that its "sustainable" products now represent 30% of its global sales.

material. In the first phase, the Holcim team aimed to make up new cement and concrete with up to 20% reused "construction and demolition material," compared to maximum 5% previously. It worked. The new material it had conceived was structurally strong and safe as 100% virgin material.

Once the product existed in a lab environment, it still needed regulatory approval. That, too, took several years. First, a new waste management law had to be approved by the Swiss national authorities. Next, the regulatory bodies in various cities had to implement new product standards. And finally, Holcim's brand new Susteno product, had to be certified for use in building and construction. By the time that happened, more than five years had passed since the initial request from Eberhard, and the company's global environmental push was in full swing. Susteno launched at a small scale in 2018, and in 2021, during the COVID pandemic, it was approved for use in larger scale infrastructure.

At this point, the global Holcim team started taking note. Most of their solutions thus far focused on the carbon part of the equation. The Swiss team's Susteno solutions, however, added a component of circularity, and a care for nature. Although, or perhaps because the pandemic was in full swing, visitors from the global headquarters started flocking to their nearby Swiss subsidiary. "I was very surprised, but it was good to see how open the group was [to our product]," Clemens marveled. When we showed our product, there was immediately a lot of interest, especially during 'Corona' times." It was a rare turn of luck indeed. While COVID has shut down almost all international travel from early 2020, hopping from Zug to Zurich was still relatively easy. The towns are less than half an hour apart by train. "It was the right place, and the right time," Clemens said. "Everything converged."

★ ★ ★

Soon after the Swiss visits, Jan and his executive team floored the accelerator on their global decarbonization strategy. Based on its sustainability levers, in July 2020, Holcim launched Eco-pact, a type of concrete with a reduced CO_2 footprint of at least 30% compared to standard concrete, in the US[12] and 25 other countries.[b] In 2021 and 2022, further additions to the eco range of products followed, including Ecoplanet, Holcim's green cement with a reduced carbon footprint, and Ecocycle, a range of recycled products directly inspired by the Susteno recycling brand. In Altkirch, France, for example, Holcim managed to produce a clinker "entirely made of recycled minerals," the company proudly announced in June 2022.[13] Because clinker is the main component of cement, having it made of recycled minerals bridged another gap toward being nature positive and carbon-free. And in Saint-Laurent-de-Mure, Holcim started to upcycle demolition materials into recycled cement, aggregates, and sand to get to a fully recycled concrete.

The years since have vindicated Holcim's strategy—and the Swiss innovations that helped catalyze it. Today, Ecopact and Eco-planet are blockbusters, with each posting more than a billion dollars in global sales. The eco range of products helped Holcim to record revenues and profits in 2023,[14] and by the fall of that year, almost a fifth of Holcim's global cement and concrete sales came from the eco brands. In the US, Amazon became a marquee Ecopact client, using the concrete for its new data warehouses in northern Virginia[15] and giving the brand additional credibility in Holcim's biggest market. The concrete mix used in the project there, the company said, would reduce the CO_2 footprint of the concrete by 39%.

Holcim also proved it could decouple revenue growth from greenhouse gas emissions. Its CO_2 emissions per ton of cement produced dropped by 29% since the 1990s, the company calculated. The company has also diversified its product mix. Since 2020, CO_2 emissions per dollar of net sales at the company have

---

[b] The official names of the Holcim products listed in this section are ECOCycle®, ECOPlanet, and Susteno. We've used simplified spelling for readability purposes.

dropped by 43%—the result of a combination of higher prices, a further lowering of the CO_2 intensity of its cement and concrete, and greater sales of other, less CO_2-heavy building products, as well as the several divestments. And thanks to the company's science-based targets, which Magali first championed, Holcim is now doing its part to limit global warming to 1.5 degrees Celsius between now and 2050, rather than the more than 2.5 degrees pathway the world is on now.[16]

But for Holcim to become a truly circular company, even more aggressive progress will be needed in the form of systems change, the company also knows. Getting on the sustainability track was the first challenge, and Magali, Jan, and others helped the company meet that challenge. They changed the company's overall mission, set ambitious and science backed decarbonization targets, and developed and marketed new, more sustainable products such as Ecopact and Ecocycle. By 2023, the company was "very much in operational mode," Nollaig Forrest, who succeeded Magali on the executive team, told us. "All teams are working on them. The business has been wired," she said. But as carbon-light operations have become the new normal, it is time to take an even greater leap forward, she said. "We need to take a systems approach to make sustainable construction happen at scale. It's about engaging across the building value chain with specifiers, from public authorities and urban planners to real estate investors, architects and engineers to accelerate demand for more low carbon and circular solutions."

Nollaig is one of the faces of this 2.0 approach to sustainability. And she considers that two stakeholders are crucial in this new challenge: governments and suppliers. "We need to change the regulatory environment, in every single market," she told Peter in an interview. "And with carbon capture, utilization and storage, we need to create partnerships with companies for the capturing, reuse, storage, and transport of CO_2, and have new regulation, too. What's needed is new paradigm, a new industrial framework to build up," she added.

Nollaig, who has a background working with chemical companies like Dow, Dupont, and fragrance maker DSM-Firmenich, knows how to build such alliances. Her specialty is public affairs, and it will be an expertise that will come in handy when reaching out to governments, regulators, and further ecosystem partners. It will also be necessary: the new nature of business is one where companies understand that they are part of a much larger ecosystem, to which they have to add value, rather than subtract it. The possibilities are there: the ecosystem we live in includes all other societal and economic actors, with which companies can work to create systems change. And it includes the natural ecosystem, with which companies can partner, too, by ensuring they are nature positive, rather than exploitative.

The challenge that lies ahead for Holcim's leadership is gigantic, knowing that the company's reality for decades was to be a net-negative contributor to the natural ecosystem. Companies like Holcim did exploit nature, and their product cycle wasn't closed at all. It's one thing for a company to create processes and decarbonize its operations step-by-step. It's a whole other challenge to become truly circular, and still be a growing and profitable company. Holcim will have to climb this hill, and it won't be a walk in the park. As it finds it feet in this challenge, it will also still have to account for its past and ongoing negative externalities, including its CO_2 emissions.

Despite having come a long way, the company faces quite a few detractors because of its historic business model. There is a group of Pacific Islanders from Indonesia who are suing Holcim in Swiss courts since early 2023. HEKS, a Swiss NGO that supports the islanders, said, "they are demanding compensation for climate damages they have suffered, a financial contribution to flood-protection measures, as well as the rapid reduction of Holcim's CO_2 emissions." Whether those claims will be held in court remains to be seen. Jan told Peter that he preferred to focus on the future, rather than the past. But the fact that cases like this pop up, shows how the road to a decarbonized world can get tricky if you were previously on a different track.

We nevertheless commend Holcim for its reinvention. It is a company that shows how you can adopt the new nature of business, all while continuing to play a major role in global economic growth and development. Its playbook tracks the one we describe in this book. By aiming for decarbonization and circularity, Holcim shows it wants to work with nature, and not against it. By setting science-based targets, it gives directionality and guard rails to its overall objectives. And by showing ambition at the top and allowing for initiatives to come from the bottom up, it exemplifies the type of leadership we like to see.

If it succeeds, Holcim will also contribute to the double objective of our model, which is about both sustainable *and* inclusive prosperity. The sustainability element should hopefully be obvious by now. The inclusive aspect comes from remaining a company that builds for the many, and with many people. Holcim has more than 60,000 collaborators worldwide, which go from blue collar operators at its quarries and kilns, to white collar executives such as Miljan Gutovic, Nollaig Forrest and Jan Jenisch, as well as local leaders such as Clemens Woegerbauer and Cathleen Hoffmann.

The story of Clemens and Cathleen also embodies another lesson about inclusivity: that to succeed in the 21st century, you cannot count on your internal resources alone. Success comes from deeply listening to your customers, going into your value chain, and coming up with solutions that work for everyone. It also comes from seeing governments and regulators as partners, rather than adversaries. Finally, the inclusion at Holcim can be found in the destination of its construction material products, which are used in buildings for all members of society, going from state-subsidized housing in France, to the sustainable school in Vienna, Austria, and 3D printed houses in Kenya.

In Chapter 8, we will look at two companies that have taken even more radical steps in the journey toward sustainability.

Innergia, a Swiss energy start-up, built sustainability and inclusion into its business model from the get-go. It creates renewable energy locally, with the local population acting as consumers, shareholders, employees, and guardians of the company's energy production. And the second company, Schneider Electric, a French multinational, has been on a journey of complete transformation. When it was founded, it operated mines and produced weapons. Today, its purpose is to help companies use less, but more sustainable, energy.

Chapter 8

A Whole New World of Business Opportunities

"They are like Saudi Arabia," James Gentizon said. "They have plenty of energy."

James, a Swiss engineer and entrepreneur, wasn't talking to us about a new oil field in the Middle East or the Americas. No, he was talking about Rossinière, a small, Swiss, Alpine town in the canton of Vaud.

At first sight, though, Rossinière looks nothing like Saudi Arabia. It's one of those typical picturesque Swiss towns surrounded by mountains, reachable only by a small road or train. Geographically, it's about halfway as the crow flies between Montreux at the shores of Lake Geneva, and that most famous of all Swiss towns: Gruyère, known for its delicious cheese.

So, what had James so excited about Rossinière, then? As it turned out, it was wood. "There is 1,000 hectares of wood," he said, pointing to the forests all around the town center. That wood, he said, could the town's answer to the two wicked problems facing its people—and those around the world: human-made climate change, caused by the burning of fossil fuels, and the decline of democracy, caused by all kinds of forces, including the concentration of economic power in the hands of just a few individuals and companies. In Rossinière, the abundant presence of wood could solve these challenges on a micro-scale. And if his project succeeded there, it could quite likely succeed almost anywhere in the world, he believed.

In Chapter 7, we saw how existing, large businesses like Holcim can rethink the role they play in the economy and be a net positive force for society, as former Unilever Paul Polman would say. We saw how Holcim reflected on its relationship with nature, and how it tried and democratize its new business model so that it works for all. In this chapter, we want to go a step further. We want to show how the new nature of business can be almost the opposite of the old nature of business. It can promote broad prosperity, rather than devolve into a game of winner-takes-all. It can truly act in balance with nature from the get-go, rather than operate in a parallel reality. And it can use technology to the benefit of humankind, rather than in one company's narrow self-interest, which often is at odds with that of society.

To make this point, we will tell the story of two companies: James's Innergia (an energy start-up in which André has invested), and Schneider Electric, a French multinational company whose business model today is almost the opposite from what it was almost 200 years ago, when it was founded.

★ ★ ★

You can speak to Jean-Pascal Tricoire everywhere in the world. While writing this book, we saw him in Geneva for breakfast, as he got ready for the chairmen's retreat of the World Economic Forum. We talked to him over the phone when he was in Hong Kong (his company, Schneider Electric, has developed a truly global presence, and Jean-Pascal wanted to be where the market was fastest evolving—so he relocated to Asia in 2011). And we even chatted with Jean-Pascal while he was in Bourg-Saint-Maurice, in the French Alps, where he likes to go kayaking and feel one with nature.

Wherever he is in the world, though, Jean-Pascal has Schneider Electric in mind, and the role it can play in the world. Its purpose is to "empower all to make the most of our energy and resources, bridging progress and sustainability for all."[1] In practice, it means Schneider is a specialist in both saving energy and in making sure the consumption of energy does not cause any unnecessary burden to the planet.

To say Schneider Electric didn't start out this way would be an understatement. The company had its start in France's industrial revolution, when Adolphe and Joseph-Eugène Schneider bought an iron foundry in the small but burgeoning town of Creusot, in France's Burgundy region. It was the start of a success story that largely tracked that of the industrialized world. In the 19th century, Schneider became an industrial giant in iron ore production, and its downstream applications: steel, industrial machinery, railway equipment, shipbuilding, and even weapons. Schneider's growing success attracted many people from around the region and France at large to join the company. In Le Creusot alone, the population grew from about 1,500 just before the Schneiders arrived, to a high of just under 40,000 a little under a century later.

But as successful as the Creusot ventures of the Schneider brothers and their successors were, we know now that they also had a darker side. Steel production has been one of the key contributors to global CO_2 emissions from the 19th century to today, the weapons Schneider and others produced heralded in the era of total warfare and destruction in the 20th century, and the industrial lifestyle of the past two centuries largely was at odds with living in harmony with nature. None of that is *specifically* Schneider Electric's fault, and our knowledge about these darker sides of industrialization only developed with time. It would be unfair to retroactively blame it on them. But had Schneider continued its business model of the 19th and early 20th century into the 21st, there would be very few positive things to say about this industrial giant.

It's a good thing then, that Schneider Electric changed its ways. As so many companies, Schneider went through a facelift the latter half of the 20th century. It engaged in all kinds of mergers and acquisitions (M&A) activities, oftentimes as the buyer, but just as often as the party being bought or sold. What emerged from this turbulent era, was a company almost unrecognizable from the one it had once been. In the early 1980s, notably, the steelworks in Le Creusot closed, understandably leading to a stir in the region. During that same era, due in part to government pressures, Schneider divested most of the activities that had made it an industrial giant to begin with, as well as its banking and telecom activities. What was left of the company centered on electric equipment, such as switchboards, electric power plants, and industrial electronic systems.[2] It was this heavily changed company that Jean-Pascal Tricoire joined at the end of the 1980s, as part of one of the company's mergers.

Jean-Pascal was a young manager at the time, and few in his hometown might have suspected he would go on to transform one of France's largest multinational companies. Jean-Pascal hailed from Beaupréau, a rural town in the country's western Loire region, the son of farmers. He had spent his entire youth in the town of 6,000 and loved the countryside lifestyle. Even while he was studying to become an engineer, he returned home every weekend until the age of 23.[3] But when he joined Schneider Electric, he became a global citizen almost overnight. Jean-Pascal's first decade at Schneider brought him to Italy, China, South Africa, and the US, as the company was all in on the 1990s globalization wave. By the early 2000s, he got tapped for the top job, first as COO in 2003, and then as CEO in 2006. What was he going to do with the company? What was its DNA, after all the M&A, the divestment of its original business, and the embrace of globalization?

"The very early vision we had," Jean-Pascal told us, "Was that the global energy model was not sustainable." Schneider Electric, with its roots in coal and steel, and its current business in the electricity market, was in a good position to realize this earlier than most, perhaps because of its serendipitous history. It had added *Electric* to its name at the end of 1999 to reflect that it had left behind its carbon and industrial legacy in the preceding years and was now going all-in on electrical solutions.

The new business model gave Schneider and Jean-Pascal a front row seat in what was happening in the energy market. On the one hand, its leading market position in switchboards and electronic systems gave the company an intimate understanding of how energy was used in houses, offices, industries, and cities. Schneider learned very quickly that a lot of energy was wasted by its customers, such as when lights were left on with no one present, or heating remained turned on when buildings were empty. It also saw how digitizing the management of electricity systems could easily lead to energy savings in this regard. As the 1990s gave way to the 2000s, advances in IT made this ever more possible.

On the other hand, Schneider's engineers knew firsthand how polluting fossil fuels were as a source of energy—and how much better "clean" electricity was. "The very clear picture we had, through our historical asset, was that electricity was the only path to decarbonization," Jean-Pascal told us. But having led the industrial revolution from rural France also meant that Schneider wasn't going to hate on traditional sources of energy any time soon. The same was true for Jean-Pascal: "With my rural origin, I could see the deadlocks caused by a lack of energy. Energy is your passport to a decent life," he said. "But energy also has damaging effects, like pollution in cities, and environmental damages."

Just about the time Jean-Pascal took the reins of Schneider, these two mega-insights came together: namely, that at the intersection of digitization and decarbonization lay a beautiful, big business opportunity. Or, as the engineer Tricoire put it, "When you plug those two together, digitization and clean energy, you realize that big electrons marry very well with small electrons."

Although the whole energy debate and industry was and is still focusing on supply—coal, oil, gas, solar, wind, nuclear—Schneider focused all its forces and technologies on the energy transition on the demand side. It observed that we would not exit the "age of fire and carbon" by starving the world of fossil supply but by helping all to transition out of fossil addiction, reducing the need for energy with more efficiency and replacing fossil combustion with more clean electricity. This positioned Schneider strategically for the next 20 years as the champion of the transition of energy demand, preparing well also the landscape for electric vehicles and heat pumps.

Thus started a 20-year journey that saw Schneider quadruple its revenues, multiply its market value tenfold, and become recognized as the most sustainable company in the world,[4] all while helping its clients degrow and decarbonize their energy consumption. In financial terms, Schneider today has global revenues of €36 billion ($39 billion),[5] net income of about a ninth of that, and a market capitalization of about €121 billion ($131 billion).[6] It is a curious and impressive fact, that you can *grow* from promoting *degrowth* (in energy), and that you can become *more profitable* from becoming *more sustainable*. But it is also a proof point for our thesis: that the new nature of business is about sustainability, inclusivity, and prosperity, all at the same time. Let's look at Schneider's transformation a bit more in detail still.

Just before Schneider's exponential growth path began, the company made a landmark decision: in 2003, it joined the UN Global Compact. "Back then, only a few companies were part of it," Jean-Pascal recalled. But for Schneider, it felt like the right thing to do. In practice, it meant that the company subscribed to helping achieve the Millennium Development Goals, the precursors to the Sustainable Development Goals, and that it intended to put sustainable development at the heart of the company. But why did Schneider do it? Today, its arguments seem commonplace. But in

2003, they were still novel. Said the then CEO, Henri Lachmann, "Climate change and the efficient use of natural resources are the most important challenges, both now and in the future. We're fully aware of the stakes and intend to help build a sustainable world by providing customers with environmentally friendly products and solutions."[7]

The company was aware of the stakes of climate change and the use of natural resources, but it was also aware of the opportunities. "Climate change is 80% due to energy issues," Jean-Pascal told us, looking back at the strategic shift. "You can address it either by aiming for higher efficiencies, or by decarbonizing through electrification, or better yet, by the combination of both." At the time, the idea that doing more with less was a contrarian insight, as "bigger is better" fossil fuel energy and car companies were still by far the largest companies in any industry: in 2004, for example, Exxon (no. 2), Chevron (no. 6), and ConocoPhillips (no. 7), were all in the top 10 of Fortune 500s list of largest US companies, and so were General Motors (no. 3) and Ford (no. 4).[8] But the notion that there was growth in efficiency and electrification did at that point become the kernel of Schneider's growth engine. "Customers saw the interest, because if you save energy, you save money," Jean-Pascal said. "And you become more able to operate in countries where energy is scarce."

It led to myriad products and market moves—and a lot of sustainable growth.

First, Schneider moved from being a company heavily reliant on its European home market, to a truly global one. In the US, where energy is typically cheap and abundantly available, its growth was fueled by a small but growing demand for cleaner and more efficient energy, and huge needs for automation and digitization. That demand first came from pioneering companies, such as Schneider's fellow Global Compact members. But by today, it has morphed to include almost the entire economy, as decarbonization, energy efficiency, and digitization have become watchwords for just about every company, thanks to the Paris Agreement and net-zero pledges by groups of companies. Consequently, during Jean-Pascal's tenure, Schneider's revenues in the US grew fivefold.

The biggest growth story for Schneider, however, occurred in the Asia Pacific, where the company's footprint grew eightfold. China, Southeast Asia, and India, notably, saw their economies take off in a series of miracle growth stories. But unlike the energy-rich regions such as the US or the Middle East, energy in most of these markets was always scarce, expensive, and in the case of fossil fuels, imported. It made Schneider's offering of energy management attractive from the get-go. Schneider's software enabled companies to monitor where they used most energy, and where savings were possible. And its emerging consulting services could help companies plan future energy uses, including the development of renewable infrastructure, heat pumps, or other cost- and carbon-saving efforts.

In terms of its business model, Schneider evolved from making only the old-school switchboard and other analog products, to offering myriad digital software solutions, and then from providing data to providing insights and advice, including sustainability consulting services. At Peter's vacation home in Chamonix, France, for example, you can still find a classic Schneider switchboard, which enables one to turn the electricity on and off in various parts of the home. But the much larger part of Schneider's business today is to help corporate clients electrify their energy needs and to help them save on their energy bill by finding efficiencies and savings through digitization and software.

Organizationally, the company went from being centrally led from France, to having multiple hubs, including in Asia and the US, and having a local culture wherever it operated. It also streamlined its IT infrastructure—which was initially a hodgepodge of legacy software systems—to aim to trend to one, globally operational system. And in terms of its approach to people and culture, it went from attracting engineers and other product-focused individuals to attracting global talent based on Schneider's leadership in sustainability.

All along, though, the company never stopped being agile, rational, and metrics-based with a long-term profit motive in mind. "We readjust our portfolio constantly," Jean-Pascal told us. "We've acquired and developed consulting and services, but at the same time, we've taken $2 billion worth of revenues out of our portfolio. We have a venture capital arm to invest in green shoots and new companies. Some succeed and some don't.

Finally, Jean-Pascal insists that despite the company's sustainability makeover, Schneider still respects its legacy. "We built our vision respecting the legacy," he told us, referring to the legacy in electrical technologies. The whole journey of transformation consisted in adding layers of new value for customers—digital, software, AI, consulting, services, full solutions, and so on—making sure those new layers would be solidly plugged in the legacy to create superior synergies and faster accelerations at scale. It also made sure the culture would be inclusive enough to bring all those new profiles and talents and enable them to thrive within the same environment.

It's an incredibly impressive transformation. And yet, even more transformational businesses exist. Enter again, the world of James Gentizon and his "Saudi Arabia" of Switzerland, in the woods of Rossinière.

★ ★ ★

James Gentizon, you could say, worships the sun, though he does so in a rational, not religious, way. To the engineer, the burning star at the heart of our solar system is the alpha and omega of our energy equation. It is the key also, he believes, in our fight against climate change. And, the sun is fundamentally a public good to which no one has a monopoly. "It may seem like there is a lack of energy," he told us. "But the first energy is the sun. Its energy is everywhere. The planet, it is only energy."

As said, James is not religious in his worship. He is deliberate and scientific: when you observe energy in its purest form, you just realize it all starts with the sun. Consider the heat that makes up thermal energy: it comes from the sun. It is this energy that makes plants, trees, and vegetables grow, and that fuels us as people. Nature transforms heat into chemical energy in living beings, or in hydrocarbons, fossilized over hundreds of millions of years. But its origin is still the sun. So it goes for other types of energy. Geothermal energy, mechanical energy, or gravitational energy—none of them would be around in the first place if it wasn't for the sun and the earth.[a]

There is a point to starting James's story with these solar considerations. Two, in fact. The first is that in this reading, a fundamental feature of energy is that it doesn't belong to any one particular person or company. Like the sun itself, energy is the ultimate global common. It's a far cry from how energy is owned and traded in our global economy, with just a handful of companies and countries dominating our current supply of energy. The second point is that solving the challenges posed by our current energy system isn't all that complicated, if you start from a perspective of energy abundance. If energy is everywhere, in all kinds of forms, you just need to pick the right method to extract it, if you want it to benefit all.

Here's how James puts it, in his own words:

What have we done? Because we are a little lazy, we decided to tap the hydrocarbon fossil fuel first [among all types of energy]. And we burn it, to turn it into thermal and electrical energy, because what we need for our economy to function is [these types of energy]. It was very simple, and of course it created a lot of additional CO_2 emissions. This is why we now have climate change. If we want to work on the cause of climate change, we must stop with this—all this fossil fuel. We need

---

[a] That's true first and foremost, because the earth wouldn't be around if it weren't for the sun: it was created "over 4.6 billion years ago out of a mixture of dust and gas around the young sun," as Sasha Warren of the University of Chicago put it (https://news.uchicago .edu/explainer/formation-earth-and-moon-explained).

to stop, and we must restore or refix this balance of biological energy. We can do it. In every village, in every small collectivity, especially in the countryside. We can do it.

There is another thing in our vision. All these energy sources are a common good. The sun is shining for everybody. No one has owner-ship of the sun. It is a public good. We think it is nonsense for energy to be like any kind of product, based on the market forces from one day to another. Why is it so? Because in our system, only a few people said, these fossil fuels, they are ours. The oil companies and [oil] states. It doesn't work. Only a few people are earning a lot of money, and [many others] that are poor and not benefiting. We can make sustain-able prosperity, but it means energy cannot be a product [like this].

It's a radical perspective, to be sure, but James's approach to sustainable and inclusive prosperity isn't a pipe dream. It is already underway in Switzerland. To see how it works, let's return to Rossinière.

In Rossinière, a sparsely populated, but vast mountain town, people have been living with nature since time immemorial. Located at almost 1,000 meters of height (about 3,000 feet), the forces of nature are omnipresent in Rossinière. Snow covers the town for much of winter (although less so in recent years, as Peter experienced during an early March visit), and the mountain pass that connects Rossinière to Montreux's Lake Geneva takes a wide bend around the Alpine Mountain peaks that enclose the town. But nature doesn't just present challenges here; it offers opportu-nities, too. Most houses in Rossinière are made of wood, sourced locally from the forests that surround the town. They are so sturdy, and so beautifully built, that they are today a tourist attraction, giv-ing visitors a taste of idyllic Swiss living. The very woods that made Rossinière so inaccessible for centuries, thus also made it possible for people to live and visit the place today.

Yet like elsewhere, the town and its people over the course of the 20th century tapped into the "lazy" source of energy provided by fossil fuels. In Switzerland as a whole, petroleum, motor fuels, and gas make up more than two-thirds of energy consumption at present,[9] and they are all imported, mostly from Nigeria, the US, and Libya.[10] Rossinière is no exception in its dependence on foreign fossil fuels, and its contributions to the CO_2 emissions that come with it. But it needn't be that way, James realized. It is at this point that he made the comparison with Saudi Arabia in our conversation, pointing to the town's plentiful supply of wood. With modern techniques, the town could be almost fully self-sufficient in filling its energy needs with that wood. The right energy infrastructure would enable Rossinière to collect wood from its forests, pyrolyze it to produce thermal energy and electricity, supply its people with district heating, and provide electricity to the grid.

The benefits of such an approach would be countless, James said. First, and most important, it would make the town largely net-zero in terms of its carbon emissions. Cutting trees and turning the wood into gas would emit carbon of course, but as new trees would be planted each year for the ones that were cut, the forest of Rossinière would be able to recapture the released CO_2, creating a circular energy system. Just as important, though, would be that the energy system would be fully homegrown, creating local jobs, and ensuring supply at preset prices. Between 60% and 80% of the town's energy needs could be supplied locally, James estimated, with the remainder taken care of by the "backbone of the Swiss energy system," including its nuclear and hydro power. Finally, in James's plans, the energy company delivering this energy would be almost entirely locally owned, by the town's people and government. That in turn would create a financial prosperity loop, in which the benefits of the town's energy production go back to the town and its people.

This vision is now becoming reality. In 2022, the municipal council of Rossinière approved to act as guarantor for the energy plant proposed by James, to the tune of over 10 million Swiss francs ($11 million).[11] A few months later, André stepped in as investor in James's Innergia Group, the company that would create the energy infrastructure of Rossinière and other towns that choose for its solutions.[12] With the financing secured, the building blocks of Rossinière's future energy system are now in place. In the next phase, the town will organize a referendum, and ask its citizens if they approve of the plans. In the proposed setup, the municipal government and a private citizens' cooperative would together control 98% of the local energy company. The last 2% would be owned by a privately held company set up by James,[b] which in turn would make a services agreement with Innergia. It would allow the latter to earn back the initial investments it makes in the project and give it the means to finance and organize daily operations for a duration of 20 years.

Innergia's initial energy project in Rossinière, as well as a similar one in another Swiss town, won't revolutionize the Swiss, let alone global, energy market, on their own. But the principles that guide the new company are groundbreaking, which is why we support them. The most important element of projects such as Innergia's is that they make energy production and consumption *sustainable*. The various carbon capture techniques used in Rossinière would reduce the carbon footprint of the town's energy production by 99.99%, James calculated. Moreover, by creating a tight link between production and consumption, these projects ensure local ownership and prosperity. Yet unlike some energy systems of the past, or those in certain countries, the setup in Rossinière is still liberal and capitalist in nature. A large part of the energy production would go to a municipal system of district heating, but the electricity that is produced would go on to the national grid, with its variety of suppliers and buyers. And although the community controls most shares in the company,

---

[b] By organizing the governance of the energy infrastructure in this way, Gentizon told us, a double objective would be met. On the one hand, with 98% percent of the shares in the hands of the people and government of Rossinière, it would be clear that the project is meant to benefit the community. On the other hand, by having 49% plus 2% technically in private hands, the newly established company would not be legally a public company, avoiding the complex laws on public finance.

technically, 51% of shares does nominally remain in private hands (albeit with a public benefit).

It is not hard to contrast this approach to energy with the one we currently have. In the US and Europe, for starters, five historical "super-majors" dominate the oil and gas sector. BP, Chevron, ExxonMobil, Shell and TotalEnergies in 2022 had combined revenues of over $1.5 trillion, and together rewarded their shareholders with dividends and share buybacks of more than $100 billion,[13] making them among the largest companies in the world. Elsewhere in the world, the energy sector is equally consolidated, with state-controlled companies such as Aramco (Saudi Arabia), China National Petroleum (China), Petrobras (Brazil), ADNOC (United Arab Emirates) similarly among the largest and most profitable energy companies. Together, these and other major oil and gas companies are responsible for the lion's share of global carbon emissions of the past 100 or more years. And although many of them are today partially publicly listed, the profits these companies make still only benefit a small part of the global population, considering that the harm on which these profits is based affects the entirety of the planet.

★ ★ ★

For our global economic system to be sustainable and inclusive, we need more companies like Innergia, and fewer companies set up like the super-majors. Energy should be treated and traded more like a global common than like a privatized good with mainly financial features. And it should be handled with care, especially when it comes to its net carbon footprint. We need the planet to provide resources for many generations to come. Digging up and burning fossil fuels without compensating for their CO_2 footprint doesn't fit in that picture. For all these reasons, we should use more of the business design principles of Innergia and stop providing licenses to operate to companies that have the exact opposite approach.

All this doesn't mean that large energy or industrial companies must disappear. To the contrary. As the transformation of Schneider Electric shows, some of the greatest positive changes in our economic fabric can come about when a large industrial company decides to change its ways. Schneider's start in the 19th century wasn't any different from that of any of the companies that became super-majors over time: it exploited a coal mine and burnt CO_2. But as the company reflected on its mission throughout the 20th and 21st centuries, it changed its ways. Today, the company still helps the greatest number of people get access to energy. It is more successful in delivering on that purpose than at any other point in its history. But the means it deploys to get there is completely different. That is thanks to a variety of changes, starting with making the Millennium and Sustainable Development Goals its north star, and ending in developing an expertise in how to save energy and use renewable sources instead.

If Schneider can change, so can any other company in the world. It opens a whole new world of business opportunities for companies, new and established. It is worthwhile—even necessary—for others to pursue those opportunities, too.

Chapter 9

The New Nature
of Leadership

"**L**et me dive right in," Anne-Fleur Goll said, kicking off her graduation speech at one of France's most famous business schools, HEC Paris, in June 2022.[1] "After a few months of carefree campus life, I felt deeply upset, realizing that the careers it was leading me to, were the main cause of [the planet's] environmental collapse. I learned both about marketing and the negative impacts of overconsumption and greenwashing. I saw the same companies at career fairs, and in polluters' rankings." The crowd, made up of hundreds of fellow graduates, burst into spontaneous applause.

This was not an education or career trajectory Anne-Fleur wanted to be part of, she continued. She didn't want to be a cog in the wheel of an unsustainable economic system. So, during her studies, she had made a choice about her career, she told her captive audience. Together with many other of her fellow students and recent graduates, she had become part of the "Movement for an Ecological Awakening."[2] The group demanded that "companies should be prepared to place the ecological perspective at the heart of their organization and their activities."

More than anything, the group made a pledge about themselves: "As citizens, as consumers, as workers," they wrote in a manifesto, "we affirm we are determined to change an economic system in which we no longer believe. We know that this will imply changing our way of life . . . [But] we are prepared to make [ourselves] available with enthusiasm and determination . . . we want to encourage all actors in society . . . to play their role . . . and to make the changes necessary to a finally sustainable society."

When Anne-Fleur finished her speech, she got a standing ovation. Clearly, she had said what was on the mind of many. It didn't take long for media to take notice. Leading French publications such as *Le Monde*,[3] *Le Point*,[4] and radio channel France Inter[5] all reported on her speech. It was noteworthy because Anne-Fleur was not making her claims from the sidelines. She was the representative of her class, and her school was among those educating the elite business leaders of the country. Even the *Financial Times* dedicated a piece on Anne-Fleur and her message.[6] What does Generation Z, the generation born between the mid-1990s and 2012, want from their education and career, the piece asked. Interviewed, Anne-Fleur said she wanted business schools to "be the grown-ups" and to truly take the lead on topics such as climate change, degrowth, and planetary boundaries.[7] A few hours talking about sustainability or diversity wouldn't do, she said.

Back in Fontainebleau, a town southeast of Paris, Katell Le Goulven nodded in agreement. Katell had joined INSEAD, one of the most renowned graduate business schools in the world,[8] after a long career at the United Nations. As inaugural director of the "Hoffmann Global Institute for Business and Society" (set up with an endowment from André), her job was to do what Anne-Fleur and others now also demanded—and what André had long believed was necessary for the new nature of business to become reality: to fully integrate sustainability in the business school curriculum. Katell didn't have to start from scratch—the conversation and the academic research on the evolving role of business in society had been going on at INSEAD for decades, she told us.

But when the institute got started in 2018, the mandate grew to "bring it to the next level."

★ ★ ★

As the UN climate meeting in Dubai, UAE, progressed in December 2023, Halla Tómasdóttir and the leaders of The B Team started to grow worried. The B Team, a group of business leaders concerned about the "well-being of people and planet,"[9] as they put it, and of which Halla was the CEO, had been working more than a decade to show that business could play a positive role in addressing the world's greatest challenges. Virgin founder Richard Branson, Harley-Davidson CEO Jochen Zeitz, IKEA's "Ingka Group" CEO Jesper Brodin,[a] Thrive Global CEO Arianna Huffington, and former Unilever CEO Paul Polman were among the group's leaders, changing the course of their own business, and motivating others to do the same. (André, too, is among The B Team's 30-some "leaders."[b]) But as business, civil society, and governments met in the Dubai emirate late 2023 to discuss climate change at a "conference of the parties" (COP), the feeling among The B Team leaders was that things were headed in the wrong direction.

Initially, many participants and observers had hoped the COP would end with a landmark agreement on the phaseout of fossil fuels. They hoped that it would herald the start of a new era geared toward a greener economy. Encouraging statements by the president of the meeting, the Emirati politician (and former national oil executive!) Sultan Al-Jaber had suggested that was indeed the ambition. "The world has reached a crossroads," he said in his

---

[a] The company most of us know as IKEA is separated into several legal entities. Ingka Group is the one that operates IKEA's retail stores in 31 countries and is responsible for 90% of global IKEA retail sales. Footnote (e) will explain this in detail.

[b] The group prefers the term *leaders* to merely *members* for those who are part of The B Team to underline the responsibility they have to display leadership.

opening remarks at the summit. "The science has spoken. . . . We feel, as you feel, the urgency of this work. . . . I ask you to start this COP with a different mindset. . . . No issue is left off the table. And yes, as I have been saying, that includes the role of fossil fuels."

But as draft agreements started to trickle in, it became clear that negotiators *were* considering leaving out the crucial notion of an end to fossil fuels. That would be a disaster, The B Team felt, as it would end all hope that the world could limit global warming to 1.5 degrees Celsius, the ambition previously set in the COP's Paris meeting eight years earlier, and a crucial threshold for maintaining life on earth as we know it, according to most scientists.

Halla expressed the sentiment that reigned among them in those early days of December 2023. "The COP had started with some ambitious statements, to the surprise of many," she told us, referring to Al-Jaber's words. "But then there was a lull, this 'die down' of ambition that also always happens in global meetings. People started to think 'this is not going to happen.' Hope was lost, and doomsday thinking, as well as distrust started to bubble up. Momentum was vanishing. The whole ability to believe in a positive outcome, the mindset and mood, was not there. Increasingly, there was suspicion about fossil fuel lobbying."

Halla and her partners from many organizations across the climate movement didn't want to give in to that pessimistic outlook. They gathered at a breakfast meeting on the sidelines of the meeting in Dubai and came up with a plan to reinsert crucial passages into the COP agreement. The breakfast was convened by Global Optimism, a climate advocacy group cofounded by former UN climate chief Cristiana Figueres[10] (and a fellow B Team leader as well) alongside their partners at Systems Change Lab, Bezos Earth Fund, and The B Team. "We decided to rally around a strong call," Halla said. "We needed to choose who we were going to be. If we were going to lose the ability to show up with courage [at COP28], then we were going to lose the critical years to deliver on the just transition to a 1.5 degrees Celsius world. We had no time to lose. We called upon our negotiators to include a signal to transition away from or phase down fossil fuels [in the final agreement] and get back to believing in science," Halla explained.

Coming out of the breakfast, the coalition, which began referring to itself as *Team Courage*, wrote an open letter asking Sultan Al Jaber and all parties "to deliver a 1.5C aligned outcome [at COP28] in response to the Global Stocktake—because later is too late."[11] They reiterated previous demands for a tripling of renewable energy by 2030, a doubling of energy efficiency, and, once again, the phaseout of fossil fuels. With the letter drafted, B Team and the other members of the informal coalition immediately went to work. They asked everyone they knew to sign and share the letter, hoping that in this way they could influence the final COP agreement. The power of the initiative, Halla said, was that no single organization owned it alone, yet many people from across the movement went above and beyond to land it. But even Team Courage was surprised by what happened next.

★ ★ ★

In the previous chapters, we showed how companies are adopting the new nature of business in their strategy and operations. They adjusted their business models so they could be in line with nature, or they came up with entirely new offerings that were inclusive and sustainable from the get-go. But even when pioneering companies adopt these new ways of doing business, we cannot be sure that systems change occurs. Showing that a new nature of business agenda can work and be profitable for an individual company is inspiring, for sure, but it doesn't guarantee that everyone follows suit.

Today, we are still faced with a system designed for an era when the consciousness about nature and inclusion wasn't as widespread. And our education, especially that of business leaders, is by its nature slow to adapt to the latest thinking about sustainability. To change that, we need leaders who go beyond their own business agenda and work toward broader systems change.

Such systems change requires moving all the pieces that make up our societies to end up with a new system that behaves in a qualitatively different way.[12] The stories of Halla and her allies at The B Team, and Anne-Fleur and Katell and their efforts to reform business education, are perfect examples of people and organizations working toward such systems change. They are also efforts André has been involved in on a personal level. They embody the "leadership" aspect that is required to get to an economic system of inclusive, sustainable prosperity. Let's explore them further.

★ ★ ★

For The B Team, the attempted Hail Mary in Dubai to keep the 1.5 degrees Celsius limit to global warming alive wasn't the first time the group made itself known. The collective had been founded more than a decade earlier—on June 13, 2013. Since its inception, The B Team was premised on the very idea that you need business, government, and civil society to come together to "help get on top of some of the world's seemingly intractable challenges,"[13] as the organization's cofounders, Richard Branson (known from founding Virgin) and Jochen Zeitz (who had rose to fame as CEO of Puma) put it at the time. For these founders, it had been clear for quite a while that when it comes to the great challenges humanity faces, "not every company can do it alone," as Jochen, told us in an interview for this book. The necessity to decarbonize the world, together with the need to maintain biodiversity, are two important factors that define planetary boundaries, Jochen said, and they are challenges that are out of the reach of pretty much any individual company.

Jochen had experienced the limits of what one company can do when he experimented with the concept of an "environmental profit & loss" (EP&L) as CEO of sportswear company Puma, a role he held for almost 20 years until cofounding The B Team. (When he started in the role, in 1993 at age 30, he was the youngest CEO of a publicly listed German company.[14]) "Puma is an animal that lives in the wild," he said about the company name's double meaning, "so I wanted to know what our environmental impact was [as a company]." Measuring Puma's *full* impact on global biodiversity was not possible, as the company's day-to-day operations were too far removed from that much larger reality. But the company *could* measure its impacts and dependencies on water and land use, so it put these in its first EP&L. "Having that overarching understanding of where your impacts are is absolutely critical," Jochen said.

The results were sobering, but actionable. Puma's first ever EP&L valued its (negative) impact on the environment at €145 million (about $159 million), the exercise revealed.[15] About €91 million ($100 million) came from greenhouse gas emissions and water consumption, and €51 million ($56 million) from land use, air pollution, and waste.[16] But knowing what its impact was, was just the first step.[c] Thanks to the report, the company could now do something about it—and it did. For example, "we did away with the trusty shoe box and replaced it with the 'Clever Little Bag,'" Jochen wrote in an article for *The Guardian*.[17] "This meant we used one million [liters] less water a year, 8,500 [tons] less paper (as much as the combined weight of 1,400 elephants), and reduced energy consumption equivalent to a small town's." In the more than a dozen years since that first EP&L, including after Jochen left in 2012, Puma took many more steps to address its footprint. Still, despite these best-in-class efforts, which led to a decline in Puma's relative environmental impact (impact over sales) Puma's total environmental impact kept increasing over the years.

From a systems thinking perspective, efforts at making improvements at the individual corporate level are laudable, but not very

---

[c] In fact, the euro valuation of Puma's environmental impact changed over the years as the company's accounting methodology evolved. What mattered more than knowing the euro value, then, was to see whether or not the impact increased or declined in comparison to Puma's evolving sales.

impactful. What matters much more is that our entire economic system evolves to stay within planetary boundaries. "We can have emissions, even climate change, but it can't breach the boundaries that alter the state of our planet," Jochen told us. "With 8 to 9 billion people we have to find ways to consume and give planet the ability to regenerate. It doesn't mean that net-net all businesses are positive. The sum of it must be positive."

It is precisely at this level—the aggregate one—that the work of groups such as The B Team were meant to make the difference. As Jochen told us, "It is the role of governments and politicians to set a framework." But doing so, especially in a sustainable and inclusive way, is easier said than done. Just like companies don't automatically pursue a higher purpose than making a profit, governments won't automatically come up with frameworks that enable positive systems change, or that force the global economy to operate within planetary boundaries. And that is because just like any organization, governments are imperfect. The people that lead them have their own backgrounds, experience, interests, connections, and blind spots. And just like any other group of people, they rely on those around them to best advise them what the best plan for the future of society and humanity could or should look like.

Jochen Zeitz and the Reinvention of Harley-Davidson

Jochen continued his journey of creating the new nature of business at Harley-Davidson, the iconic motorcycle company, which he first joined as a board member in 2007. Jochen was an avid biker himself and knew from the get-go that the Harley community was a very particular one: aficionados of the brand love making long, "easy rider" journeys on their bike, have a sense of freedom and adventure among their community, and get a kick from the roaring sound of their bike's internal combustion engine. If Harley was ever going to become sustainable, switching out its legendary motor for an electric one was probably not the best place to start—and in any case, when Jochen joined the Harley board, even Tesla had yet to release its first ever electric car, the Roadster.

Either way, the more immediate challenge facing Harley-Davidson at the time of Jochen joining the company wasn't its environmental footprint. The Wisconsin-based manufacturer had just come out of a major union strike when Jochen took on his board seat, and in the years that followed faced an extremely treacherous external environment. From 2008 to 2010, the American automotive industry almost went belly up following the global financial crisis, and several Detroit-based manufacturers had to be bailed out by the government. Harley fared slightly better but was still forced to cut over a quarter of its Wisconsin-based workforce.[18]

The years that followed brought ups and downs for the firm. In the years to 2014, Harley came roaring back following a revival of the US economy and expansion in the bustling emerging markets of Asia and South America. Its stock, too, came soaring back to precrisis highs. But in the five following years, Harley slid back once more. Harley's core customer base, the rebellious baby boomers, started to enter the twilight of their bike-riding days, consulting firm Roland Berger suggested.[19]

The challenges facing Jochen looked like a labyrinth, with each turn the company took seemingly leading to another dead end. To stay relevant to a new generation of consumers, for example, Harley needed to come up with a compelling electric bike offering. But LiveWire, the electric motorcycle brand Harley had been developing since the 2010s, met with resistance from Harley's existing customer base. They valued the features of the classic, fossil-fueled Harley much more, including

(continued)

(continued)

the long range of its fuel tank and overpowering motor sound. But Harley couldn't build a future based on any "Make America Great Again" type of strategy, either, appealing to Trump, his policies, and his voters because "the politics of motorcycle enthusiasts are as diverse as the ways in which they customize their bikes," The Guardian's *Jill Rothenberg observed at the height of the Trump years.*[20]

And then there was the immediate, unsurmountable problem in front of Jochen as he took on the job of CEO in the early days of March 2020: the oncoming COVID pandemic. Whatever the company came up with, the reality was that it was forced to a standstill. For almost three months it could not produce any bike, meaning its sales dried up just as the company needed new money.

For Jochen, though, the perfect storm Harley faced was not a deterrent to take on the hands-on CEO role. "I was willing to do it because I always look at a crisis as an opportunity," he told us. But where was he going to start? On a personal level, Jochen believed in creating nature-based economies. He had proven as much at Puma (and also in Kenya, where he runs a wildlife conservancy and related businesses as a personal project). He also saw a need for Harley to think 10 years out, and that meant developing a successful technology that would end up in an electric range of bikes. Yet his leadership agenda at Harley started with an entirely different priority: uniting Harley's riders and employees in times of hardship. "Especially in the context of COVID, we all had to unite," Jochen told us. "We had to come together to fight the pandemic. So, we established this rallying cry: 'United We Ride.' It came out of us shutting down our factories, and coming together as a team with our customers. We had to find solutions and head forward. Coming into the business, it was the right thing for me to do."

"United We Ride" also helped address Harley's other "social" challenge: after years of political division in the US, the company and its diverse set of stakeholders wanted to find common ground behind

a nonpolitical message. "You have to find a way to bring people together, rather than dividing them," Jochen commented." When we say, 'United We Ride,' that's exactly what we're promoting. Harley is a positive community. When you ride, you are part of the tribe. It doesn't matter where you're from. That's the glue that brings Harley riders together. In a divided world, this is about community."

The message of unity wasn't just a slogan, either. It helped Harley management and employees prepare together for a restart of their production facilities, once the COVID restrictions were lifted. And it also prepared the ground for the next step in the financial recovery of the firm—which cemented the inclusive nature of the company going forward. In 2021, Jochen made more than 4,500 employees stockholders of the Harley-Davidson company through an equity grant at the start of his five-year "Hardwire" strategy. "It aligned the interests of all employees, from factory workers to executives, to benefit when the company succeeds," Jochen told us, pointing also to how it fit in Harley's broader "Inclusive Stakeholder Management" approach.[d] "Essentially, everyone became a shareholder," he said.

Jochen may have focused on the "social" side of the equation first, but he didn't forget about the company's environmental impact. Already as a board member, he had been pushing the company to consider the climate reality in which it operated, and its responsibility in it. Now, as CEO, he was tasked to implement it. But he was stuck between a rock and a hard place. On the one hand, "electrification on four wheels" was in full swing by 2020. Electric cars, an eccentric and futuristic prospect when Jochen joined as board member of Harley, were now a reality even in Motor City and Munich. The need to

(continued)

---

[d] For Harley-Davidson, committing to inclusive stakeholder management means "helping transform our business by ensuring we have positive impact on people and the planet while continuing to deliver profit for our shareholders," Jochen Zeitz said in the company's inclusive stakeholder management report 2022. The full report is available at https://investor.harley-davidson.com/governance/sustainability/.

(continued)

turn away from fossil fuels was just as pressing for motorbikes. On the other hand, the Harley all-electric LiveWire bike wasn't immediately a runaway success. It didn't have the range Harley enthusiasts were used to, was pricey, and seemed to attract a more urban rider as core customer. Jochen himself liked riding both a LiveWire and a traditional Harley, but he seemed to be one of the only ones.

Jochen realized he couldn't push the electric motor on to his customers. Nor did he want to. But he was also convinced that investing in an electric range was important on a 15-to 20-year horizon, including for Harley-Davidson. "You have to think about the longer-term future," he said. So, he decided on a dual strategy. Harley-Davidson would continue to prioritize the internal combustion engine for all its branded motorbikes, for now. But LiveWire would also continue to exist, and even become a fully-fledged brand in its own right. "Rather than under the Harley umbrella, we made LiveWire a separate brand that could operate under its wings, and act as an agile start-up that could lead electrification," Jochen said.

Under the new plan, executed in September 2022, LiveWire became a separate listed company. It could more aggressively pursue its all-electric future, with an ambition to become carbon-neutral by 2035, and appeal to its own environmentally conscious customer base. But synergies between it and the Harley mothership would remain. The two companies have a shared services agreement, in which software development and manufacturing were shared. And Harley also retained an important shareholding in its spin-off. "Everyone still understands LiveWire is part of the Harley family," Jochen said. That way, once the technology is ready, Harley will have the option to shift into its electric gear faster than its competitors.

Jochen's approach at Harley won't please everybody. But to Jochen, it is important that although the direction of travel is the same for every company, the speed at which you can go, and the actions you can take, depend on your specific set of stakeholders. "The need to decarbonize the world is not a trend; it is a necessity, embraced by the world, so you can look at leading the electrification as a life insurance or an opportunity, either way you would want to be ahead of the game," Jochen said. But when you translate that necessity into a business plan, he also said, "you have to create win-wins, not at the expense of someone." The nonprofit he runs in Kenya, and the publicly listed Harley-Davidson company, he clarified, "share a common vision, but apply strategy and actions in a different way." "Keeping all stakeholders in mind is important to be successful in the future," he said. "I have always looked at the long run, and that is how businesses need to be run. You can't achieve everything in a few short years. Society changes over time. And those [changes] happen long term. That's why strategy always has to be anchored in the longer-term vision."

In Dubai, it didn't look like that constellation was working. Instead, lobbying from oil and gas companies seemingly took the upper hand over the longer-term interests of humanity. According to one review, more than 2,400 people with ties to fossil fuel industries were registered to attend the COP meeting in Dubai.[21] The B Team felt that the voice of more short-sighted leaders was winning out versus that of leaders with a more "multistakeholder surround sound" perspective, as Halla described it. It was why the organization and its partners decided to step in and step up. "We felt that we had to use our collective voice to influence governments and peers," Halla said. "We wanted to lead by brave action and catalyze courageous leadership." And so, Team Courage came into being. The core initiative the group took was to publish its open letter (see box). But every individual and organization involved took it on themselves to amplify the letter in their own way. The ripple effect all those contributions caused in just a few dozen hours was enormous.

The Transformation Is Unstoppable. An Open Letter to COP28 President Sultan Al Jaber, December 8, 2023, Dubai

Dear COP28 President Sultan Al Jaber,

As we enter the final days of COP28, we are at a tipping point.

The world and its people need the strongest possible outcome to keep 1.5 degrees within reach. But delivering on this historic task requires us to act like a team.

The signals of transformation and opportunity across sectors and society are all around us. At the same time, the climate emergency is biting harder than ever. It's up to us to seize this opportunity—because what is achieved here in Dubai must mark a legacy moment which determines the fate of our future generations.

We—CEOs, mayors, governors, investors, Indigenous peoples, health professionals, young people, faith leaders, scientists, athletes, and more—stand in courage and resolve with the COP28 President and all Parties in bringing us together behind a rapid response plan to the Global Stocktake.

To reach this positive tipping point, we know we need the following:

- *An orderly phase out of all fossil fuels in a just & equitable way, in line with a 1.5C trajectory—whilst ensuring the tripling of global renewable energy capacity by 2030 from 2022 levels and the doubling of energy efficiency*

- *The enabling environment to scale up and shift public and private finance, with developed countries taking the lead in action and support; putting a price on carbon and tripling investments for renewable energy*
- *The halt and reversal of deforestation and land degradation as well as biodiversity & other ecosystem loss by 2030 and safeguarding the territories of indigenous peoples; ensure resilient food systems and deliver a strong global goal on adaptation*

These outcomes must be supported by the implementation and ratcheting of Nationally Determined Contributions and National Adaptation Plans well before COP30 in 2025 which align with 1.5C and incorporate multi-stakeholder efforts within them.

Later is too late.

Yours,

First, there were of course the signatories from The B Team itself, including the CEOs of IKEA, Salesforce, Chobani, and Natura, in addition to Andre, Jochen, and Richard (Branson). On the corporate side, 400 more business leaders signed, including the CEOs of major global companies such as Danone, Uber, Heineken, Nestle, McCain Foods, Philips, Maersk, and Patagonia, just to name a few. "We were landing signatures like crazy," Halla said. And those signatories weren't just corporate ones, either. Well-known individuals such as primatologist Jane Goodall, philanthropist Laurene Powell Jobs, adventurer Bertrand Piccard, and former New Zealand prime minister Jacinda Ardern also signed. And from there, the list got larger and larger still. Celebrities such as Mark Ruffalo, Jane Fonda, and Susan Sarandon joined in; world-renowned scientists added their name to the list; as did faith leaders, global youth leaders, the mayors of Paris and London, and the heads of more than 400 NGOs, including those of WWF, The Club of Rome, Ceres, and the UN Global Compact.[22]

Nor was the collection of signatures the only action. Fellow B Team leader Cristiana Figueres, who had convened the breakfast and founded "Global Optimism" (alongside Tom Rivett-Carnac), got to work to get the letter the most airplay possible. One critical piece was engaging with the COP president's team, who needed help raising the ambition. It led to the letter and its signatories being displayed on the massive walls outside the COP28 congress center in Dubai, for all negotiators of the meeting to see. The "We Mean Business" coalition, which gathered businesses that were similarly aligned on climate action, and that counted The B Team among its members, also published a page wide ad in the *Financial Times* in those final days of the convention, reiterating their core message to national governments that "the time has come for a fossil free future" and "later is too late."[23] Those Team Courage leaders that could also had meetings with country negotiators. The experience was eye-opening to Halla, she said. "We met with some G20 leaders in person, and really pushed," she recalled. "I remember this moment where one [key negotiator] said, 'we never have meetings like this.' And I remember thinking, oh, my god, this is how broken the system is, that governments go at it alone. Maybe governments because of populism don't have the dialogue with business that they need to. But there [can't be a limit to global warming] without business stepping up."

For all these unexpected twists and turns, the urgent efforts by Team Courage paid off. In the final days of COP28, the negotiators agreed on a text that (re)introduced many of the building blocks the collective had called for. "Countries reach 'historic' COP28 deal to transition from fossil fuels," the *Financial Times* summarized it.[24] And indeed, the final agreement called all parties to "transition away" from fossil fuels,[25] and subscribed to the crucial goals of tripling renewable energy and doubling energy efficiency by 2030, just as Team Courage had urged them to. It came as an enormous relief to the group. Since the breakfast, the core team involved had "neither been sleeping, nor letting details get in the way," Halla recalled. Now, at least temporarily, the mood was more celebratory. "There was an incredible social movement," Halla said. "Many people felt, 'we did it.' It was an effort shaped by many, and that's fantastic. We could all feel very proud of the role we played." As for The B Team, it aimed to "catalyze change," she said, so she was happy to see so many people "own" the success. "The development of the text is so much negotiation that there is no way of knowing what is in the text or not at one particular point in time. It's such a messy process," she said.

A few months later, at the World Economic Forum in Davos in January 2024, The B Team CEO did get kudos for her team's work back in Dubai. "Many people told me thank you, and said we made a meaningful difference," Halla said. But by that time, the group and its leaders had moved on to the next battle, she said, because an ambitious UN agreement is crucial to avert a climate disaster, "but we also know it's not enough." Indeed, as we saw previously in this book, real world progress today on creating a society and economy in line with planetary boundaries is far from sufficient. The world is still headed for several nature-based crises, and inequality among people is also still getting worse. It is a realization that constantly preoccupies The B Team and also one that incites them to take more action still, whether as a group or as individuals. One last example from a B Team leader and the company he leads may help clarify this point: Jesper Brodin and IKEA.

The Sustainable Transformation of IKEA, and Its Systems Change Leadership

If you're not a connoisseur, you might walk into an IKEA store today, and think nothing much has changed there in the past few decades. The IKEA restaurant still serves Swedish meatballs at a surprisingly low price, the store itself still feels more like a well-designed labyrinth than a traditional furniture store, and you still get to pick up your furniture in flat carton boxes, and build it at home yourself.

But below the surface, IKEA has been undergoing a massive transformation in the past decade or two. And to regular IKEA customers, the results are starting to show. Those typical Swedish meatballs? There's a vegetarian version of them today, and in some mature markets, like Germany, almost 40% of customers will pick these or other plant-based meals over the traditional meat-based dishes. Inside the store, heating and lighting won't feel or look any different, but IKEA today generates 150% of its energy needs through renewable energy sources it owns and operates itself. The same is true for the product offering. Hundreds of furniture products have different components, all with one common theme: they require less raw material, thereby limiting the company's ecological footprint. And in virtually every IKEA store, there is now a second-hand department, run by the company itself. You can sell your old IKEA furniture back to the chain and buy used furniture from IKEA directly. (Peter and his wife know this firsthand: they've both sold to and from IKEA's second-hand department.) Even how you get to or from an IKEA store is different now. If you're still headed for one of the Swedish retailer's traditional big box stores outside city centers, you can now do so with electric cargo-bikes provided by the company. Increasingly, though, IKEA itself is moving its stores to where its customers live,[26] opening city stores to avoid further contributing to the car-based era in which it grew big to begin with.

These developments are not a coincidence. They are part of a broader transformation underway at IKEA, which aims to make the company circular by 2030, and more specifically, in the company's own words, "to inspire and enable more than 1 billion people to live a better everyday life within the boundaries of the planet."[27] The leader who is leading the company on that journey is B Team leader Jesper Brodin, CEO of IKEA's Ingka Group, the company running 90% of global IKEA stores[e] (going forward we'll refer to Ingka as simply IKEA.). Just like so many other leaders, he didn't start his career with sustainability in mind. But over time, as he learned more about the global economic system and IKEA's role in it, he decided to adopt a sustainable and circular mindset, and make it his own.

When Jesper started working at IKEA in the 1990s, a sense for adventure and challenges is what drew him in. Jesper's first assignment was to find new sourcing opportunities for IKEA textile in South Asia, and the sky was the limit. "When I joined IKEA in Pakistan in 1995, the business case was incredible," Jesper told us. "We broke through a frontier. We went from 1% of IKEA textile made in Pakistan to 30% in 2.5 years." The founder of the Swedish retailer, Ingvar Kamprad, liked what he saw. The thrifty Swede was still very much an active force in the company when Jesper took on his first job. Kamprad loved a good deal, Jesper recalled, and had a deep interest in finding ways of sourcing IKEA products at lower costs

(continued)

---

[e] Jesper's team clarified that "Ingka Group is the world's largest IKEA retailer, with retail operations in 31 markets, representing about 90% of IKEA retail sales. It is a strategic partner to develop and innovate the IKEA business and help define common IKEA strategies. Ingka Group owns and operates IKEA sales channels under franchise agreements with Inter IKEA Systems B.V. It has three business areas: IKEA Retail, Ingka Investments, and Ingka Centres." More info at https://www.ingka.com/this-is-ingka-group/.

(continued)

elsewhere in the world—provided the quality remained the same. Jesper offered the company just that.

    Less than three years, Jesper moved to what could become an even more promising market: Indonesia, one of the world's largest exporters of wood products.[28] *Jesper was once again tasked to develop product sourcing in this Southeast Asian country, as well as in neighboring Malaysia. It was a specific assignment for a specific employee at a specific company, but it also happened at the backdrop of a broader macro-economic development: the rapid globalization and liberalization of the global economy in the 1990s and early 2000s. In those years, we know now looking back, globalization reached its historical apex. The economists and policymakers that advocated it, saw in this trade a source of ever-expanding global prosperity. More than 200 years earlier, the Scottish economist Adam Smith had first talked about trade, comparative advantages, and the increasing "wealth of nations" in the early days of the industrial revolution. Now, in the eyes of institutions such as the World Bank, this logic was bound to come to full fruition. Economies in emerging Asia, such as Indonesia, would gain from producing raw materials and selling them at low prices to the West; advanced economies such as Sweden or the US would gain as well, because their consumers could purchase goods at lower prices than if they were made or sourced locally.*

    At IKEA, Jesper in Indonesia, and Kamprad back in Europe, saw the theory play out in practice. The inexpensive textiles from Pakistan and inexpensive wood from Southeast Asia helped IKEA deliver on its promise to offer well-designed products at "prices so low that as many people as possible will be able to afford them,"[29] *and to lower their prices over time. The Smithian logic even worked both ways. Not only did IKEA source from these lower cost countries, it also opened stores. In the 1990s, IKEA opened retail stores in*

Malaysia, China, and Poland,[30] for example, turning those countries into both production and retail markets. The rising trade tide was lifting many boats indeed. But Kamprad, Jesper, and others also started to realize there was a darker side to the trade story. What did the sourcing of IKEA products do to the environment? What were the working conditions of IKEA's new suppliers, and what happened further down the value chain? "At that time, we didn't know, and didn't even have a point of view on whether we were responsible," Jesper told us, looking back at those early days of his career. With his experience in some of these new source countries, Jesper joined Kamprad and other executives in the discussions centering on a key question: "Do we limit our [social and environmental] responsibility to ourselves and our offices? Or can we have only one set of values?" The latter point of view won out, and IKEA's first global code of conduct, the IKEA way, or "IWAY" was created[31] in 1999. It stipulated 10 principles and dozens of specific requirements, all with the overarching aim to improve the company's environmental impact, secure decent and meaningful work, respect human (and children's) rights, and improve animal welfare.[32]

Over the next few years, as he led the implementation of the code of conduct in countries like Indonesia, Jesper learned one of the most important management lessons of his life, namely, that "it is good business to be a good business," as he put it. "It is true, over the years, some suppliers discontinued their relationship with us," Jesper told us. He also acknowledged that the early days of IWAY were a bit like a step in the dark, especially in emerging markets. "Initially, the code there wasn't ready," he said. "There were still questions on how the implementation should happen, and what the cost consequences should be." But when push came to shove, and it was time to implement the code, Jesper said, "to my surprise, most suppliers reacted positive." One of the defining moments, he said, happened when

(continued)

(continued)

he was in the room with a group of producers. "In the dialogue, two groups were forming," Jesper recalled. "One said: 'IKEA you have to make up your mind. Do you want low cost, or sustainability?' whereas the other said, 'Do you want a low price? Then you have to work on sustainability.'" The opposing groups touched on a nerve, as Jesper and his colleagues had been dealing with the same conundrum themselves. "It was this deep dilemma," he said. "We're building this amazing company. But does it do good for the world? When we added the code of conduct, we feared the business part would suffer."

But as the IKEA executives found out, this was a conundrum that wasn't. "The exact opposite was true," Jesper told us. "The nature of economics is that waste is cost," he said. "So the respectful use of resources is a good idea." Reducing externalities such as waste or pollution led to reductions in costs. In a way, that realization was nothing more than the modern version of what a young Ingvar Kamprad had already known when he started out after the Depression and the Second World War in rural Sweden. "At IKEA, our founder came from an environment where thriftiness was not an ethical topic, but the way to make a living," Jesper remembered. In the Kamprad's family farm, like in any of its neighbors, no food or wood went to waste. Why should the economic logic be any different now? Over time, Jesper's understanding of the positive interplay between sustainability and "good business" extended to the workforce, too. He came to see the positive relationship with a motivated (and fairly remunerated) workforce, a purposeful job, innovation, and excellence. "High motivation drives excellence in any company," he said. "For companies that survive, technology and innovation are main drivers. The application of modernization is the success factor of the big brands. It's not systemizing abuse."

Yet, as IKEA woke up to their social and environmental impact and responsibility, another blind spot remained, Jesper told us: the impact of business and people on climate change. As Jesper rose through the ranks at IKEA, he remained largely unknowing on the topic that would come to dominate the global agenda a mere decade later. "Until 2007, 2008, I was unaware. . . . We had no clue on climate change," he told us, referring not just to himself and his company, but the broader ignorance in society. As the science became increasingly clear, however, and the impacts of climate change started to be felt around the world, Jesper started to worry more, and feel guilty for any further inaction on his behalf. "I'm increasingly concerned," he said. "In hindsight, I feel personal responsibly to be part of fixing what our generations and the generations before have caused. I look at my kids and their future. They are well aware of what we and I do."

It made the new nature of business agenda personal for Jesper. When he got elevated to CEO of Ingka Group in 2017, the UN had just two years earlier agreed on the Sustainable Development Goals to be achieved by 2030. In Paris, another UN Conference of the Parties had reached a landmark agreement to try and limit global warming to 1.5 degrees Celsius. Such high-minded goals for human development gave Jesper the impulses he needed to build on IKEA's strategy around becoming "people and planet positive" by 2030, which had initiated in earnest a few years earlier.[f] If it succeeded, it would be good business, he knew from prior experience. It would also be a great motivator for all the company's stakeholders, including its suppliers, employees, and customers, he also found. And, it was a corporate mission Jesper himself deeply believed in, and that gave him hope and motivation for himself and the next generation.

(continued)

---

[f] IKEA's "people and planet positive" strategy had been adopted by IKEA's management team for the first time in 2012. It was then led by sustainability manager Steve Howard. Before that, Anders Dahlvig, IKEA CEO from 1999 to 2009, had worked on sustainability as part of his "never-ending to-do list" of IKEA, the IKEA team informed us. It meant that Jesper "stood on the shoulders of giants" when he decided to build on IKEA's sustainability strategy.

(continued)

So how did he fare? Fairly well indeed. In the years since taking charge, Jesper proved just how far a new nature agenda can go, he shared in a note to his fellow B Team leaders in January 2024. Since 2016, the year of the Paris Agreement, IKEA's business grew by 30%, he wrote, while the company's absolute carbon emissions fell by almost a quarter. "I [realize] this might sound like blowing our own IKEA-trumpet a bit loudly," he said in his note. "But my point in sharing it with you is merely to say that here is one of an increasing number of examples that 1.5 C is possible and that it truly is good business to be a good business."

By the time we were finishing this book, in spring 2024, Jesper invited us to a roundtable in the Netherlands at RetourMatras, a company that IKEA has invested in. As the name suggests, RetourMatras recycles mattrasses. For IKEA, the investment in the company was and is part of its systems approach to solving challenges. IKEA is the largest producer of mattrasses in the Netherlands, where RetourMatras is based, but the company accepts any mattress, including non-IKEA ones. In fact, RetourMatras has the capacity to recycle all 1.5 million mattresses that are disposed in the country each year.[33] The roundtable Jesper invited us to, went even further: it discussed which policy environment is needed to support the circular economy in the European Union—beyond mattresses, and beyond the Netherlands. The company also unveiled its expansion plans to new markets as it has just opened in the UK and is planning for France after summer.

At IKEA, CEO Jesper Brodin elevated the company's own new nature track record. He decoupled the company's growth from its carbon footprint. He also pursued initiatives that helped reduce the use of natural resources, limited waste, and recycled previously used products to give them a second life. (See preceding box.) Such a focus on action fits with the moral compass of The B Team. That compass, which Halla developed shortly after becoming the group's CEO in 2018, made it visually clear what the team and its individuals stood for (see Figure 9.1). At the heart of the compass are humanity, and the key goals of sustainability, equality, and accountability. On the edge are the key characteristics The B Team expects of its leaders: have a purpose and combine it with principles. And be both bold and brave at the same time. "To be bold means to think outside of the box, or even to think without a box.

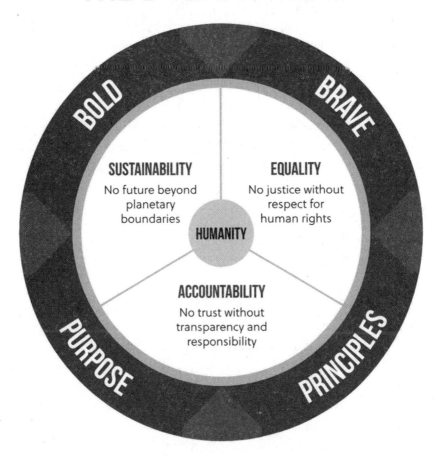

Figure 9.1   The B Team compass.

Source: The B Team, Our Mission. https://www.bteam.org/who-we-are/mission

We have to challenge the conformity that brought us here," Halla said. "And to be brave means standing in service of something that is bigger than you."

Similar to other B Team leaders, Jesper embodies the team's moral compass. IKEA's purpose under his leadership has evolved to include the bold dream of becoming a circular company, as its investment in circular economy company RetourMatras highlights. And Jesper is brave, too. As CEO of a major multinational, he could easily limit his leadership to his company, which has an extended enough reach as it is. But as the new nature agenda is personal to him, he expands his leadership to people and organizations beyond IKEA. At the SDG Tent in Davos in January 2024, Jesper organized an "Action Speaks" breakfast, where he first shared his company's progress on climate and nature, then invited other CEOs, such as H&M's then CEO Helena Helmerson, to share theirs, and finally challenged everyone in the room, to come up with climate actions at their respective organizations. Jesper also organizes intergenerational gatherings within IKEA. The meetings bring together youth and seasoned executives and came into being "to talk about the courageous future that we want, but that we hadn't yet catalyzed," Halla, who attended one of them, said.

Jesper's and IKEA's journey is in that way a great example of what The B Team does, beyond "catalyzing courage" in the world. Halla says it best:

For individual leaders, being part of The B Team brings a sense of community in a world and a system that is not necessarily in service of humanity. The system is so misaligned with what is in their own heart. [In The B Team], they find a community of support, and more importantly, peer accountability. When someone shares [results like Jesper's at IKEA], it is not to blow your own horn. It is to say: not only is it possible, but it is also happening. When The B Team leaders hear from each other, they learn from each other. They call on each other. I've seen it again and again. Being a leader in a broken system is incredibly hard. Being part of a community that sets the highest bar, is very much a way for personal responsibility. I wouldn't underestimate how important it is to be on a team like this. When someone is braver than you how it is pushing you also. Every CEO should have a B Team of sort. Because courage is a team sport.

★ ★ ★

A similar effort to have business leaders focus on "systems change," societal leadership, and courage is underway in business education. To learn how, let us return to the story of Katell Le Goulven and Anne-Fleur Goll.

By the time Katell heard the call for reform of business education by Anne-Fleur and the Movement for an Ecological Awakening, she had been working on changes at INSEAD for some four years. She had joined the school after 20 years at the United Nations and other international institutions, where she had worked on "sustainable development" from before even the term got mainstream adoption through the SDGs. "[Sustainable development] is all I've done my whole career," she told us. She researched the nature of "global public goods" at UNDP, worked on integrating climate change in official development assistance with the Swedish government, advised the UN Secretary General's Panel on Global Sustainability in New York, was a first-row witness to the creation of the UN Sustainable Development Goals in 2015, and created UNICEF's first foresight unit.

But as she worked on the public policy and multilateral side of global challenges, she started to realize something in the relation between the public and private sector didn't quite track. "There was a distribution of labor mindset," she said. "The responsibility for society and its public goods was with government, and the responsibility for private goods and profits was with the firm. As time went by, she realized this "division of labor" was suboptimal at best and extremely harmful at its worst. "We created this dichotomy that didn't have to be," she said. "Private corporations can and should contribute to the public good." Then, there was the rise of "global public bad problems," as she called them: spread of infectious diseases, pollution, the global financial crisis.

In all these global challenges, business played (some sort of) a role. If the UN or national governments wanted to be effective in addressing them, those very companies would have to be part of the solution, too. Avant-garde business leaders such as Paul Polman of Unilever understood that and became part of the UN agenda starting in the 2000s, through programs such as the UN Global Compact. "Increasingly the private sector was present, for good and for bad," Katell observed. It was a development she encouraged, but that she felt needed a more structural underpinning. So, when INSEAD called in 2018 with the offer to head its new Institute for Business and Society, she didn't hesitate.

INSEAD, then led by Dean Ilian Mihov, had long promoted the concept of "business as a force for good." And in recent years, Ilian had started to believe sustainability was central to this aspiration. The dean had little doubt about *why* this was the right approach. "It is now clear that we must change the fundamental ways that we live and grow if we want to enable more than eight billion people, and future generations to come, to thrive on a healthy planet," he wrote in the school's sustainability report in 2021. And in this systems transformation, leadership by academic institutions such as INSEAD was indispensable: "The INSEAD community possesses huge potential to lead in this transformation," he wrote. It would cause a snowball effect, where "teaching business as a force for good at all schools will change the future."

But to have conviction and clarity of purpose is one thing, to bring it to life in an entire academic institution is another. To get there, INSEAD needed to *scale* and *structure* the ways businesses and their next generation of leaders could contribute to society. The logical next question it needed to answer was *how*? Katell was happy to explore any possible answer.

Both for André and the leadership of his namesake institute, one thing was intuitively clear as they took on their mission: if INSEAD was going to change the way business worked, creating an optional "green" or "ethical" MBA in addition to the existing one was off the table. "We felt that we should not create anything in parallel," Katell recalled. "We wanted to do it as an integrated part of the whole. André wanted to change the curriculum, and we also suggested integrating [sustainability] in the research, outreach, alumni engagement, and operations of the school." It was a bold and brave goal, as The B Team would say. And it meant Katell, Ilian, and others in the INSEAD leadership team who were convinced of the cause were going to have to buckle up. Not only is academic reform by its very nature a long-term process but also it wasn't even clear at the time that all the school's faculty, staff, and external stakeholders were on board with the changes to begin with.

It wasn't even that INSEAD was *particularly* resistant to change; it is just that academia has conservative forces baked into their design, Katell said. Research is highly specialized and academic promotion is mostly driven by decades of publication in similarly specialized academic journals. Any uprooting of that specialization could mean losing 20, 30 years' worth of expertise and reputation. More broadly, she said, the highly influential rating and ranking system of business schools normalized metrics for excellence. That's a good thing because it fosters transparency and comparability. But it has also made it harder for business schools to pursue change. In fact, it could even be damaging for one school to pursue reform on its own because it would risk moving away from these homogenous references of quality and excellence—and mean the school would lose spots in the ranking. (For INSEAD, that kind of threat was particularly relevant: since 2014, it ranked consistently in the top five in the FT ranking of global MBAs, one of the most influential rankings. It reached the top position in 2016, 2017, and 2021, and has remained in the top three since.[34])

But in collaboration with faculty and staff champions, Katell persisted—aided early on by a determined dean, as well as staff who saw the writing on the wall due to the changes in society and among their students from around the world. The vision that was driving this group of changemakers was that companies should

intentionally aim to make net positive contributions, with executives up and down the value chain buying into that vision. "It is
about integration," Katell said. "It is a deep analysis of how value is
created by the firm." And if companies had to integrate sustainability in all aspects of their organization, then so, too, did the business
school for the world that taught its leaders. Working off a five-year
plan, Katell and the institute embarked on an integrative strategy.
Respecting academic freedom meant that they couldn't force any
faculty member to change their research and teaching, but they
had the advantage of a sustainable source of funding for research
projects and teaching innovations, a growing interest of the faculty,
students, and alumni, and of feeling a wind of change in society
that was pushing them on.

A watershed moment occurred when Dean Ilian brought up
sustainability in his call for a curriculum review at the school's bian-
nual faculty retreat in 2021. "The question was relatively open,"
Urs Peyer, dean of degree programs, and a participant of the meeting told us. "It could have been about the structure of the program, the length of courses, or the content of the program." Urs,
a traditional professor of finance with a PhD from the University
of North Carolina, wouldn't have been the first in line to call
for a radical reform of the MBA curriculum. But he too sensed
that change was afoot. "There was of course the external world,
that sent clear signals that business plays a role in transitioning to
something more sustainable," he said. "But there was also a lot of
research and discussion within INSEAD, thanks to André's gift,
that allowed us to articulate better what everyone is doing." The
meeting ended with the mandate Katell had been hoping for: a
select committee was tasked to show how INSEAD could integrate sustainability more closely in its MBA curriculum. Urs was
appointed its head.

The creation of a curriculum review committee was, of course,
a great interim success for Katell (and the vision of the Hoffmann
Institute). But with the review committee underway, the fate of
the integrative sustainability strategy did now lie in the hands of a

group of academics who weren't necessarily bought into the idea as much as she or Ilian was. The committee interviewed a long list of INSEAD stakeholders, going from students to recruiters, and from faculty to alumni. In the end, it put forth two options for the curriculum review: either INSEAD could leave the core curriculum as is, but mandate sustainability in one to two electives. Or the whole curriculum could be overhauled, with sustainability elements included in every core course, as well as the capstone project. For Katell, it was clear which option should prevail. The same was true for Dean Ilian (of whom Urs said that he "really [was] the driver behind the changes in education and research at INSEAD"). But despite their influence, the choice wasn't Katell's, nor even Ilian's. Curriculum review was a hefty matter, so it was put to a vote of INSEAD's entire body of faculty. Which side would they choose?

Even with all the stakeholder interviews he had done, Urs, a voting member, and an influential one at that, wasn't immediately certain about which side to back. He had heard good arguments in either camp. "It was a hard division," he said, looking back. He gave the example of the recruiters he had spoken to. "[They] wanted to have the depth of knowledge, and they didn't initially care about the breadth of sustainability," he said. "If you hire someone for privacy at YouTube, you need a specialist. That was part of the trade-off." However, as dean of degree programs, he had noticed that sustainability had outgrown the specialization category. "We found that students choose sustainability electives anyways," he said, noting that 80% of MBA students picked an elective even if it wasn't mandatory. The additional impact would not have been that great. It was this matter that sealed the deal for him. "That's where the decision to have it integrated dominated," he said. "We wanted to have it upfront, and at the end, so that there is an arch pedagogically." The vote was split, but clear: the "sustainability integration" strategy won out.

The impact of the decision was gigantic, and its historical nature was immediately clear to Urs. "We've never mandated anything in a core course in 60 years," he said. "It was always decentralized. Doing it in this way was revolutionary. You will find no other school that mandates to do something in every core course." For the faculty themselves, it meant they had to get out of their comfort zone. From one year to the next, they mandated themselves to integrate sustainability, a topic many of them had little research experience with, into their own courses. "It was a journey for me, too," Urs said. He keenly observed the changes his colleagues were making. In the accounting course, for example, students now learn about alternative metrics of measuring impact, such as a company's CO_2 footprint or its impact on biodiversity. "One of the concrete examples is you want to show your customers to show what your sweater is made of, and where it comes from, and what implications does that transparency have in the back end," he commented.

In the finance course, students look at a case in energy transition. Throughout the case, Urs said, "you start to realize that the value created for society of energy transition is in the trillions and trillions." But traditional finance calculations wouldn't show you that. "If you just apply finance to understand how that transition works, where brown energy shuts down, and green energy shoots up, you [conclude] it doesn't pay from a standard profit of view," he said. So instead, in the sustainability-infused course, students get to understand every stakeholder's position, and then create solutions that enable brown energy owners to not lose money by shutting down. The way to do so, Urs said, "is essentially from the value that society gets through health and employment." "You need to find public private financial industries to make it work and ramp up green energy." By going through the course in this holistic way, he said, "you've learned something about finance. You've identified the key bottlenecks, and you think of creating financial tools that realize trillions of benefits."

★ ★ ★

When Anne-Fleur Goll delivered her remarks at her graduation at HEC in Paris, in June 2022, she could not have known which changes were underway just a few miles further, in Fontainebleau. But anyone who starts an MBA at INSEAD today would experience a very different curriculum than the one Anne-Fleur went through in her master's degree. "This bet on the integrative strategy has paid off," Katell said. From their first day on campus, through all their core courses, and up until the capstone project that takes place over a day and a night at the end of their learning journey, INSEAD MBA students are now infused with sustainability on their way to becoming a business leader. It is a seismic departure from how MBAs are conceived historically, and elsewhere in the world. It's an observation shared by *Poets & Quants*; the online publication specialized in advising MBA candidates for their choice. "For its commitment to a groundbreaking and comprehensive integration of sustainability into its curriculum, INSEAD is *Poets & Quants'* MBA Program of the Year," the site announced in December 2023.[35] It came too late for Anne-Fleur, but on time for tens of thousands of future business leaders who will go through the INSEAD program in the years to come. It is systemic change—and leadership—at its best.

Epilogue

The previous chapters demonstrated that our current economic system is not fit for purpose, and that the status quo is no longer tenable. Humanity's future on the planet is at risk. Our value creation mechanism, which has brought prosperity, is outstretching planetary limits in a nonsustainable way. Commerce and industry must become net contributors to the system. But we also showed how a different approach is possible, and how some companies are already leading the way. In this epilogue, I want to add some thoughts to close out our book.

In its most basic form, management can be defined as taking over the responsibility and control of the individual household (*oikos* in ancient Greek means "house," and *oikonomos* means "household management"—whence the English word *economy*). The family, the property, the house was the first stepping stone for the development of our civilization. It is the basic unit of society and led to the architecture of society as we know it. First came the

---

This chapter is written in André's voice.

individual, followed by the family, and eventually, the tribe. Each step of that journey increases the difficulty of the management task.

We all have experience of how family governance can be complicated, and there are countless examples of failures in the matter. The tribe leads to the village and to the region, the country and eventually, the empire. Each step of the process is a minefield, and the rate of success tends to decrease with size. The complexity of handling these agendas is huge and, as a result, over the years, we have, as humanity, lost track of our planetary boundaries. It is important to react and to interrupt the sequence repeated here:

Individual—family—tribe—village—country—empire—collapse

To prevent societal collapse in our time, it is necessary that we bring nature back into our lives. Into our lives? Yes, into our lives—and not (even) just into our business dealings. Everything we are and do depends on nature, and nature is in serious decline. The air we breathe, the water we drink, and all the prosperity we enjoy are based on biodiversity. We ignore this at our peril. This is not just about value creation but also about our social and human condition. Indeed, our interaction with nature should and could be mutually beneficial.

As soon as humans entered the planet's evolutionary scene, they had to treat life on the planet with respect because their survival depended on it. But with the emergence of technology and societal solidarity, this permanent threat decreased substantially. Fear of nature—perhaps even ignorance about it—rather than the love for nature, became the norm. Yet nature does not have to be an enemy; it could become an ally. It *is* an ally. It is not necessarily a "cost," either. The sooner we start realizing nature's potential to create long-term sustainable value—as the cases we described in this book demonstrate—the better.

The capacity of societies to distance themselves more and more from nature, in an attempt at protecting themselves from it, has encouraged, maybe even made possible, an institutional violence against it. The "survival of the fittest" theory that Charles Darwin coined,[1] has encouraged a "winner take all" mentality among humans. This is inherently not sustainable. Physical violence has been the catalyst of a social order based on strength, where domination is the norm. Sharing is seen by many as a weakness. Our social structure is pyramidal. Some people own too much, and to them, change is not welcome.

This domination system is also at the origin of gender non-parity. The concept of the male as hunter who feeds his family might have been appropriate 10,000 years ago—though researchers question whether it was true even then[2]—it certainly does not serve us today.

History echoes through time, and the lessons of pre-collapse empires resonate in our present. Vigilance against undue concentration of power and a commitment to equity remain essential for societal resilience. Confronted with all these challenges and shortcomings, it is urgent to reassess "what we owe each other," as Columbia University President Minouche Shafik has said,[3] and to rewrite our "social contract."

This existing societal system we live in, which is formalized and rigid, stands in stark contrast with the natural world. Nature is chaotic. There is no such thing as a permanent balance in nature. Lots of simultaneous events create a multitude of short-term steadiness in an infinity of overlapping ecosystems. (That's a lot of jargon, I realize, but at least from how I look at nature, it is also an apt description of reality.) The idea of imposing on nature a linear, logical setup is inappropriate. The system is complex and has clearly resisted our repeated attempts at organizing it. Maybe we could learn from that rich reality, and not insist on trying to domesticate it. There is richness in diversity, and if we approach it with sufficient humility, we can only benefit from the opportunities provided.

The need for a holistic approach to these complex systems becomes more and more apparent. We have greatly imperiled our planet by running it like a machine, a simple system. But the reality is far more challenging. Complex systems require complex approaches. "One-size-fits-all" is just as bad as the "winner takes all" approach to managing biodiversity. These are multifactorial equations and they cannot be resolved in a linear fashion.

In fact, a single variable approach—whether "financial profit" or "carbon emissions"—will aways yield some unintended consequences. As we and others have argued, focusing on short-term profit maximization has caused a lot of long-term value destruction. Solving the whole problem with just that measure has brought us where we are.

Sadly, we are about to make the same mistake with a narrow focus on carbon emissions. This tunnel vision approach, which lets us concentrate on one single variable while ignoring all consequences, has a lot to answer for. By acting in such a rigid manner, we have deprived ourselves of the skill needed most to survive in nature: agility. Let us try to rebuild it in our system. This will make us much more resilient going forward. And resilience we will need.

There is another collateral damage of our current societal setup. Our definition of *success* is far too narrow. We have used money not just as a business indicator but also as a proxy for happiness. A full bank account allows you to indulge in "retail therapy," which will make you happy.[4] Or does it? Of course, we all need a decent and just income. We need to have a roof over our head, be able to feed ourselves well, and have sufficient means to look after our health, well-being and education. We also need savings for a rainy day or an emergency. But once those criteria are fulfilled, how much more will make you even happier? As long as we do not provide a clear answer to how much is enough, inequalities will worsen. This is a big problem, because unfair advantages and limited social mobility will lead to social unrest.

I realize that it is easy for me to engage in this rhetoric, as someone who has never had any material shortcomings and owns a lot of shares in a large and profitable company. But those privileges— and the duties that come with it—have also taught me this: The correlation between being financially well-off and leading a happy life is not a linear one. In fact, there is no constant correlation. Financial metrics, here as well, are not appropriate. Happiness is about having a sense of success—not financial wealth. And happiness has a lot to do with individual ambitions and self-realization, not with short-term satisfaction of suggested needs. The purchase of the latest fashion item or of the latest model of car will not contribute to long-term satisfaction. Yet we have constructed a whole economy based on keeping alive this niggling doubt. How long will my purchase satisfy me? Should I not make sure that my cupboard is full of the latest fashion? The same with my garage, my kitchen, and so on?

My own recipe for well-being has evolved over the years. I used to want to conform and would therefore use my purchasing power to align my shopping list to my peer group. Today, I am much more comfortable standing alone and accepting my difference. But the journey was long and sometimes painful. I feel that listing our individual frustrations and dealing with them systematically and honestly is a more worthwhile exercise than just following the crowd. I do not attempt to minimize the importance of belonging, but here, too, humility and courage are needed. A real sense of purpose will come in handy as well.

We should also analyze the peer pressure jointly with our definition of success. There is an innate desire to belong, and we are all motivated and defined by the opinion of others. There is safety in numbers, and being part of a larger group is reassuring, even exhilarating. How much are we prepared to give for being a team player? Are we willing to betray our values to do so?

I would contend that many of our fellow humans would be happier and better contributors to societies if they could be allowed to bring their values to work. Nobody should be forced to behave in a way that does not align with their beliefs. If the job and the employees do not match, the result can only be mediocre at best, and soul-destructive at worst. Doing something you do not believe in is a sure recipe for un-well-being. A job is not just a salary. It is a vital tool for self-realization and a happy life. You spend more than half your non-sleeping life at work! How do you expect to be happy if that work is unpleasant?

Feeling safe and being well-off surely add to one's sense of well-being. But if money plateaus out at a certain level in providing satisfaction, what are the alternative metrics we should use?

One important answer is that well-being does not only depend on physical well-being but also on a peaceful life. It is not surprising that humanity is suffering from "eco-anxiety," that is, a chronic fear of environmental doom.[5] We need a more resilient system to deal with the risks the future holds, and nature is the ultimate recourse, the last safety net. The natural world has evolved and dealt with change for millions of years and has been good at dealing with risk. Let us use this experience to our benefit rather than ignoring it. Here as well it is time to reintroduce nature in our lives.

At the time of closing this narrative, I feel compelled to remind us all why we need to change. We need to establish the framework conditions for the permanent establishment of a sustainable, inclusive prosperity. This is an absolute prerequisite for the ongoing success of humanity's journey on our planet.

It will not be easy and can only be described as *the biggest challenge we have ever faced*. But the societal norms we have established over the years are just that: human-defined norms. If we have established that set of rules, we can also define new ones. *Homo sapiens* is collaborative by necessity. Individual, or even couples, cannot survive on their own. Contrary to other species, we are very, *very* vulnerable in at least two aspects. First, our sleep is deep and leaves us defenseless for a big part of our lives. And second, human babies are unable to look after themselves for years. It is collaboration that enabled us to evolve into a big, brained animal. It is collaboration that has guided our evolution and has earned us the privilege of success on this planet. It is collaboration that will enable us to bring about the new nature of business.

Collaboration will always survive domination—but only if we decide so. Let us make that decision again.

Notes

Chapter 1

1. Library of Congress, "The Founding of Apple Inc.," https://guides.loc.gov/this-month-in-business-history/april/apple-computer-founded
2. Britannica Money, "Apple Inc.," https://www.britannica.com/topic/Apple-Inc
3. Academy of Achievement, "Jeffrey P. Bezos," https://achievement.org/achiever/jeffrey-p-bezos/
4. Fundable, "Amazon Startup Story," https://www.fundable.com/learn/startup-stories/amazon
5. "Google Goes Public? Search for 'Rich Get Richer,'" *New York Times*, April 25, 2004, https://www.nytimes.com/2004/04/25/us/google-goes-public-search-for-rich-get-richer.html
6. "Thiel's Founders Fund Sells Remaining Facebook Shares," Reuters, August 27, 2019, https://www.reuters.com/article/us-facebook-foundersfund-idUSKCN1VH1LO

7. The Federal, "Zip2 to Tesla to Twitter, How Elon Musk Built His Business Empire," November 1, 2022, https://thefederal .com/business/zip2-to-twitter-how-elon-musk-built-his-business-empire/

8. Brittanica, "Social Capital," July 1, 2023, https://www.britannica .com/topic/social-capital

9. Scott Kirstner, "Why Facebook Went West," *Boston Globe*, September 9, 2007, http://archive.boston.com/business/globe/ articles/2007/09/09/why_facebook_went_west/

10. Ibid.

11. Britannica, "Founding and Early Growth, Microsoft Corporation," updated January 30, 2024, https://www.britannica.com/ topic/Microsoft-Corporation

12. Paul Allen, "Microsoft's Odd Couple," *Vanity Fair*, March 30, 2011, https://www.vanityfair.com/news/2011/05/paul-allen-201105

13. Bill & Melinda Gates Foundation, Lakeside School, Remarks by Bill Gates, September 23, 2005, https://www.gatesfoundation .org/Ideas/Speeches/2005/09/bill-gates-lakeside-school

14. Hannelore Sudermann, "Before Paul Allen Funded UW's Computer Science Labs, He Got Kicked Out of Them," *University of Washington Magazine*, June 2015, https://magazine .washington.edu/feature/before-paul-allen-funded-uws-computer-science-labs-he-got-kicked-out-of-them/

15. Taylor Locke, "How Bill Gates' Mom Helped Microsoft Get a Deal with IBM in 1980—and It Propelled the Company's Huge Success," CNBC, August 5, 2020, https://www.cnbc.com/ 2020/08/05/how-bill-gates-mother-influenced-the-success-of-microsoft.html

16. Quote from Brad Stone's book pulled from "Swimming from Seattle? Jeff Bezos' Big Move Brings Us Full Circle from the Mid-1990s," *GeekWire*, November 23, 2023, https://www .geekwire.com/2023/swimming-from-seattle-jeff-bezos-big-move-brings-us-full-circle-from-the-mid-1990s/

17. "Lupin Launches US Tamiflu Generic Amid Worst Flu Season in Recent Memory," *Pharmaceutical Technology*, February 16, 2018, https://www.pharmaceutical-technology.com/comment/lupin-launches-us-tamiflu-generic-amid-worst-flu-season-recent-memory/

18. S. Ghosh, Y. Chisti, and U. C. Banerjee, "Production of Shikimic Acid," *Biotechnical Advances* 30, no. 6 (2012): 1425–30, https://pubmed.ncbi.nlm.nih.gov/22445787/

19. Atlas Brito, Anne Griffin, and Ryan Koski, "Design Life-Cycle," Nvidia GPU, accessed March 4, 2024, https://www.designlife-cycle.com/nvidia-gpu

20. Ed Conway, *Material World: The Six Raw Materials That Shape Modern Civilization* (Knopf, 2023).

21. "Natural Capital Protocol: Case Study for Roche," Capitals Coalition, accessed March 5, 2024, https://capitalscoalition.org/casestudy/natural-capital-protocol-case-study-for-roche/

22. Margaret O'Mara, "Silicon Valley Can't Escape the Business of War," *New York Times*, October 26, 2018, https://www.nytimes.com/2018/10/26/opinion/amazon-bezos-pentagon-hq2.html

23. Kevin Featherly, "ARPANET," *Britannica*, accessed January 31, 2024, https://www.britannica.com/topic/ARPANET

24. Edward Ongweso Jr., "Big Tech Has Made Billions Off the 20-Year War on Terror," *Motherboard*, September 9, 2021, https://www.vice.com/en/article/4aveeq/big-tech-has-made-billions-off-the-20-year-war-on-terror

25. Walter Hochreiter and Juris Salaks, "Roche in Basel and Western Europe," *Roche in the World: Roche in Western and Eastern Europe, 1896–2021* (Editiones Roche, 2021), p. 93.

26. "Neostigmine, Electronic Essential Medicine List," WHO, accessed March 8, 2024, https://list.essentialmeds.org/medicines/223

27. Hochreiter and Salaks, "Roche in Basel and Western Europe," pp. 142–46.

28. Walter Hochreiter, "Early Management: The Creative Mind, Authoritarian Strategist and Thinker," in Walter Hochreiter

and Juris Salaks, eds., *Roche in the World: Roche in Western and Eastern Europe, 1896–2021* (Editiones Roche, 2021), pp. 80–83.

29. "Basel Is on Top When It Comes to Culture, Quality of Life and Innovation," Kanton Basel-Stadt, accessed March 15, 2024, https://www.bs.ch/en/Portrait/cosmopolitan-basel/international-competitiveness.html

30. "About Roche Switzerland," Roche, accessed January 31, 2024, https://www.roche.ch/en/about

31. Annie Palmer, "Amazon Broke Federal Labor Law by Calling Staten Island Union Organizers 'Thugs,' Interrogating Workers," CNBC, December 1, 2023, https://www.cnbc.com/2023/12/01/amazon-broke-federal-labor-law-by-racially-disparaging-union-leaders.html

32. "Who Is the AVR," Roche Employees' Association, https://avroche.ch/en/about-us/who-is-the-avr; "Mission Statement," Roche Employees' Association, https://avroche.ch/en/about-us/vision-and-mission

Chapter 2

1. "History," World Wide Fund for Nature, accessed February 1, 2024, https://www.worldwildlife.org/about/history

2. "The Fight for Survival: Four Decades of Conserving Africa's Rhinos," WWF, https://wwfeu.awsassets.panda.org/downloads/african_rhinos.pdf

3. Geert De Clercq and Manuel Ausloos, "Mont Blanc Shrinks over Two Metres in Height in Two Years – Researchers," Reuters, October 9, 2023, https://www.reuters.com/business/environment/mont-blanc-shrinks-over-two-metres-height-two-years-researchers-2023-10-05/

4. "Der Ornithologischer Beobachter," Ala, accessed February 1, 2024, https://www.ala-schweiz.ch/index.php/ornithologischer-beobachter/ueber-die-zeitschrift

5. Christian Sampi, "Luc Hoffmann (1923–2016)," *Ornithologis-cher Beobachter* 113 (2016): 264–67), https://www.ala-schweiz.ch/images/stories/pdf/ob/2016_113/OrnitholBeob_2016_113_264_Marti.pdf

6. Walter Hochreiter and Juris Salaks, "Roche in Basel and Western Europe," *Roche in the World: Roche in Western and Eastern Europe, 1896–2021* (Editiones Roche, 2021), p. 145–48.

7. Lince Casa Rural, "Animals at Doñana," accessed February 1, 2024.

8. Trevor Kletz, *What Went Wrong? Case Histories of Process Plant Disasters* (Gulf Professional Publishing, 1998).

9. Gilbert Cruz, "Top 10 Environmental Disasters: Seveso Dioxin Cloud," *TIME Magazine*, May 3, 2010, https://content.time.com/time/specials/packages/article/0,28804,1986457_1986501_1986449,00.html

10. "Pigouvian Tax," Tax Foundation, accessed February 2, 2024, https://taxfoundation.org/taxedu/glossary/pigouvian-tax/

11. Mascham Dolly and Olga Razumovsky, *Unsere versteckten Tagebücher 1938–1944, Drie Mädchen erleben die Nazizeit* (Böhlau Wien, 1999).

Chapter 3

1. Milton Friedman, "The Social Responsibility of Business Is to Increase Its Profits," *New York Times*, September 13, 1970, https://www.nytimes.com/1970/09/13/archives/a-friedman-doctrine-the-social-responsibility-of-business-is-to.html

2. Michael Jensen and William Meckling, "Theory of the Firm: Managerial Behavior, Agency Costs and Ownership Structure," *Journal of Financial Economics* 3, no. 4 (October 1976): 305–50, https://www.sciencedirect.com/science/article/pii/0304405X7690026X

3. Economic Policy Institute, "CEO Pay Slightly Declined in 2022 but It Has Soared 1,209.2% Since 1978 Compared with

a 15.3% Rise in Typical Workers' Pay," September 21, 2023, https://www.epi.org/publication/ceo-pay-in-2022/#fig-a

4. David Autor et al., "The Fall of the Labor Share and the Rise of Superstar Firms," *Quarterly Journal of Economics*, May 2020, https://academic.oup.com/qje/article/135/2/645/5721266

5. Bronwyn H. Hall, "The Stock Market's Valuation of R&D Investment in the 1980s," *American Economic Review*, May 1993, https://www.jstor.org/stable/2117674

6. Michael Park, Erin Leahey, and Russell J. Funk, "Papers and Patents Are Becoming Less Disruptive over Time," *Nature*, January 4, 2023, https://www.nature.com/articles/s41586-022-05543-x

7. "Vitamin Makers Fined Record $755.1 Million in Price-Fixing Case," *New York Times*, November 21, 2001, https://www.nytimes.com/2001/11/21/business/vitamin-makers-fined-record-7551-million-in-pricefixing-case.html

8. Ruth SoRelle, "Withdrawal of Posicor from Market," *AHA Journal*, September 1, 1998, https://www.ahajournals.org/doi/full/10.1161/01.cir.98.9.831

9. Nicholas Calcaterra and James C. Barrow, "Classics in Chemical Neuroscience: Diazepam (Valium)," *ACS Chemical Neuroscience* 5, no. 4 (April 16, 2014): 253–60, https://www.ncbi.nlm.nih.gov/pmc/articles/PMC3990949/#ref19

10. Mahammed Juber," Health Benefits of Astaxanthin," WebMD, November 29, 2022, https://www.webmd.com/diet/health-benefits-astaxanthin

Chapter 4

1. Roche Annual Report 2008, https://www.annualreports.com/HostedData/AnnualReportArchive/r/roche-holdings_2008.pdf

2. Roche Annual Report 2022, https://assets.cwp.roche.com/f/126832/x/7cd4e2ba4c/ar22e.pdf

3. Andrew Pollack, "Roche Agrees to Buy Genentech for $46.8 Billion," *New York Times*, March 12, 2009, https://www.nytimes.com/2009/03/13/business/worldbusiness/13drugs.html

4. "Interferon," *NCI Dictionary of Cancer Terms*, National Cancer Institute, accessed March 12, 2024, https://www.cancer.gov/publications/dictionaries/cancer-terms/def/interferon

5. "Biotech Basics," Genentech, September 27, 2013, https://www.gene.com/stories/biotech-basics

6. "The Moment Two Giants Merged," Roche, https://www.celebratelife.roche.com/explore/culture/genentech-acquisition/

7. "Sustainability," Academic Impact, United Nations, https://www.un.org/en/academic-impact/sustainability

8. "The Brundtland Report," Federal Office for Spatial Development, Swiss Confederation, https://www.are.admin.ch/are/en/home/media/publications/sustainable-development/brundtland-report.html

9. "Product Stewardship," Roche, https://www.roche.com/about/sustainability/environment/product-stewardship

10. "Our SHE Goals and Performance," Roche, https://www.roche.com/about/sustainability/environment/goals-performance

11. Net Zero Targets Among World's Largest Companies Double, but Credibility Gaps Undermine Progress, Net Zero Tracker, 12 June 2023, https://zerotracker.net/insights/net-zero-targets-among-worlds-largest-companies-double-but-credibility-gaps-undermine-progress

12. Ibid.

13. "Reducing our Carbon Footprint," Roche, https://www.roche.com/stories/reducing-our-carbon-footprint

14. Ibid.

15. "Our SHE Goals and Performance, Scope 3 Greenhouse Gas Emissions," Roche, https://assets.roche.com/f/176343/x/2d01fee21e/scope-3-greenhouse-gas-emissions.pdf

16. "Roche Natural Capital Protocol Pilot Study: Application to Swiss Operational Sites," Roche, 2017, https://assets.roche .com/f/176343/x/7441be914b/not-natural-capital-pilot-study.pdf

17. "Roche Inaugurates Switzerland's Tallest Building," Swissinfo, September 2, 2022, https://www.swissinfo.ch/eng/business/ roche-inaugurates-switzerland-s-tallest-building/47872130

18. "Reducing Our Carbon Footprint," Roche, https://www .roche.com/stories/reducing-our-carbon-footprint

19. "Roche Commits to Science-Based Climate Goals," ESG Today, November 17, 2022, https://www.esgtoday.com/roche-commits-to-science-based-climate-goals/

Chapter 5

1. "Global Democracy Weakens in 2022," IDEA, November 30, 2022, https://www.idea.int/news/global-democracy-weakens-2022

2. Humanity Has Wiped Out 60% of Animal Populations Since 1970, Report Finds, *The Guardian*, October 30, 2018, https:// www.theguardian.com/environment/2018/oct/30/humanity-wiped-out-animals-since-1970-major-report-finds

3. Rex Weyler, "Limits to Growth: 50 Years Later," Greenpeace, May 1, 2022, https://www.greenpeace.org/international/story/ 53539/limits-to-growth-book-eccology-50-years/

4. "A Smarter Scenario," Stockholm University Stockholm Resilience Centre, October 17, 2018, https://www.stockholm resilience.org/research/research-news/2018-10-17-a-smarter-scenario.html

5. "All Planetary Boundaries Mapped Out for the First Time, Six of Nine Crossed," Stockholm University Stockholm Resilience Centre, September 13, 2023, https://www.stockholm resilience.org/research/research-news/2023-09-13-all-planetary-boundaries-mapped-out-for-the-first-time-six-of-nine-crossed.html

6. Chad Stone, Danilo Trisi, Arloc Sherman, and Jennifer Beltran, "A Guide to Statistics on Historical Trends in Income Inequality," Center on Budget and Policy Priorities, January 13, 2020, https://www.cbpp.org/research/poverty-and-inequality/a-guide-to-statistics-on-historical-trends-in-income-inequality

7. Anne Case and Angus Deaton, *Deaths of Despair and the Future of Capitalism* (Princeton University Press, 2020).

8. Christine Camacho and Luke Munford, "Living in the North of England Increases Risk of Death from Alcohol, Drugs and Suicide," University of Manchester, March 15, 2024, https://www.manchester.ac.uk/discover/news/living-in-the-north-of-england-increases-risk-of-death-from-alcohol-drugs-and-suicide/

9. Tito Cordella and Anderson Ospina Rojas, "Financial Globalization and Market Volatility: An Empirical Appraisal," World Bank, July 6, 2017, https://elibrary.worldbank.org/doi/abs/10.1596/1813-9450-8091

10. Mona Baraké, Paul-Emmanuel Chouc, Theresa Neef, and Gabriel Zucman, "Revenue Effects of the Global Minimum Tax Under Pillar Two," *Intertax* 60, no. 2 (2022), https://gabriel-zucman.eu/files/BCNZ2022.pdf

11. "Economic Impact of the Global Minimum Tax: Summary," OECD, January 2024, https://www.oecd.org/tax/beps/summary-economic-impact-assessment-global-minimum-tax-january-2024.pdf

12. Robert E. Scott, Valerie Wilson, Jori Kandra, and Daniel Perez, "Botched Policy Responses to Globalization Have Decimated Manufacturing Employment with Often Overlooked Costs for Black, Brown, and Other Workers of Color," Economic Policy Institute, January 31, 2022, https://www.epi.org/publication/botched-policy-responses-to-globalization/

13. "Renewable Energy, About Switzerland," Swiss Confederation, March 1, 2023, https://www.eda.admin.ch/aboutswitzerland/en/home/wirtschaft/energie/die-erneuerbaren-energien.html

14. "Renewables Share of Electricity Inches Up in Switzerland," Swissinfo, September 5, 2022, https://www.swissinfo.ch/eng/sci-tech/renewables-share-of-electricity-inches-up-in-switzerland/47876818

15. "Energy," The Government of Iceland, accessed February 15, 2024, https://www.government.is/topics/business-and-industry/energy/

16. Gavin Maguire, "Brazil Set to Widen Lead as Cleanest Major Power Sector," Reuters, October 11, 2023, https://www.reuters.com/business/energy/brazil-set-widen-lead-cleanest-major-power-sector-maguire-2023-10-11/

17. "Renewables Competitiveness Accelerates, Despite Cost Inflation," IRENA, August 29, 2023, https://www.irena.org/News/pressreleases/2023/Aug/Renewables-Competitiveness-Accelerates-Despite-Cost-Inflation

18. Ibid.

19. "Fossil Fuel Subsidies," International Monetary Fund, accessed February 15, 2024, https://www.imf.org/en/Topics/climate-change/energy-subsidies

20. "Rockfalls, Gaping Crevices Put Mont Blanc Out of Reach for Many," *Agence France Presse*, August 1, 2022, https://www.france24.com/en/live-news/20220801-rockfalls-gaping-crevices-put-mont-blanc-out-of-reach-for-many

21. "French Mayor Threatens €15,000 Deposit to Climb Mont Blanc," BBC, August 5, 2022, https://www.bbc.com/news/world-europe-62436466

22. Oscar Boyd, "The Golden Era of European Mountaineering Is Coming to an End," Bloomberg, November 3, 2023, https://www.bloomberg.com/news/features/2023-11-03/mont-blanc-mountain-climbing-under-threat-amid-global-warming

23. Ed Conway, *Material World: The Six Raw Materials That Shape Modern Civilization* (Knopf, 2023).

24. "Live Most Polluted Major City Ranking," IQAir, accessed March 15, 2024, https://www.iqair.com/world-air-quality-ranking

25. "Drinking-Water," WHO, September 13, 2023, https://www
.who.int/news-room/fact-sheets/detail/drinking-water

26. Fiona Harvey, "UN Says Up to 40% of World's Land Now
Degraded, *The Guardian*, April 13, 2022, https://www
.theguardian.com/environment/2022/apr/27/united-nations-
40-per-cent-planet-land-degraded

27. Jean-Pascal Tricoire, "Less Is More: Time to Wake Up to the
Power of Energy Efficiency," Schneider Electric, June 1, 2023,
https://www.se.com/ww/en/insights/electricity-4-0/
buildings-decarbonization/less-is-more.jsp

28. Ibid.

29. "Glass Is 100% Recyclable and Can Be Endlessly Recycled
with No Loss of Quality," Recycle Now, Waste and Resources
Action Programme, accessed November 20, 2023, https://
www.recyclenow.com/how-to-recycle/glass-recycling

30. "Glass Recycling," Sibelco, accessed November 20, 2023,
https://www.sibelco.com/en/applications/glass-recycling

31. Eliot Pernet, "How Investing in Mangroves and Sea Walls
Today Could Reduce Vietnam's Future Climate Risks by
Billions of Dollars," AXA, February 9, 2022, https://climate
.axa/how-investing-in-mangroves-and-sea-walls-today-
could-reduce-vietnams-furture-climate-risks-by-billions-
of-dollars/

32. "Insurance Solutions Can Help to Restore Mangroves as
Natural Coastal Defences," AXA, October 20, 2020, https://
axaxl.com/press-releases/insurance-solutions-can-help-to-
restore-mangroves-as-natural-coastal-defences

33. Umair Irfan, "Climate change Is Already Making Parts of
America Uninsurable," Vox, July 12, 2023, https://www.vox
.com/climate/23746045/state-farm-california-climate-change-
insurance-wildfire-florida-flood; "Parts of America Are
Becoming Uninsurable," *The Economist*, September 21, 2023,
https://www.economist.com/united-states/2023/09/21/
parts-of-america-are-becoming-uninsurable

34. Ian Smith, Attracta Mooney, and Aime Williams, "The Uninsurable World: What Climate Change Is Costing Homeowners," *Financial Times*, February 13, 2024, https://www.ft.com/content/ed3a1bb9-e329-4e18-89de-9db90eaadc0b

35. "Replanet," accessed February 29, 2024, https://www.replanet.org.uk/

36. "President Trump Signs One Trillion Trees Executive Order, Promoting Conservation and Regeneration of Our Nation's Forests," White House, October 16, 2020, https://trumpwhitehouse.archives.gov/articles/president-trump-signs-one-trillion-trees-executive-order-promoting-conservation-regeneration-nations-forests/

37. Emma Dumain, Ivanka Trump Joins House GOP to Pitch 'Trillion Trees,'" Greenwire, July 27, 2020, https://www.eenews.net/articles/ivanka-trump-joins-house-gop-to-pitch-trillion-trees/

38. Alexandra Heal, "The Illusion of a Trillion Trees," *Financial Times*, April 12, 2023, https://ig.ft.com/one-trillion-trees/

39. Josh Holder and Jeremy White, "How to Cool Down a City, Pablo Robles," *New York Times*, September 18, 2023, https://www.nytimes.com/interactive/2023/09/18/world/asia/singapore-heat.html

40. Sharon Goldman, "Sam Altman Wants Up to $7 Trillion for AI Chips. The Natural Resources Required Would Be 'Mind Boggling,'" VentureBeat, February 9, 2024, https://venturebeat.com/ai/sam-altman-wants-up-to-7-trillion-for-ai-chips-the-natural-resources-required-would-be-mind-boggling/

41. Scott L. Montgomery, *The Great Debate: When Will the Wells Run Dry?* (Chicago University Press, 2010).

42. "B Corp," Nespresso, accessed February 16, 2024, https://www.nespresso.com/ch/en/b-corp

43. "Sustainability," Nestle, accessed February 16, 2024, https://www.nestle.com/sustainability

44. "Climate Action," Holcim, accessed February 16, 2024, https://www.holcim.com/sustainability/climate-action

Chapter 6

1. Taken from Simon Caulkin, "The Rule Is Simple: Be Careful What You Measure," *The Observer*, February 10, 2008, https://www.theguardian.com/business/2008/feb/10/businesscomment1

2. "Purpose," Roche, https://assets.roche.com/f/176343/x/26a1038ed1/purposebrochure.pdf

3. "Purpose, Mission, and Vision Statements," Bain & Company, January 31, 2023, https://www.bain.com/insights/management-tools-mission-and-vision-statements/

4. Own analysis, based on the Fortune 20 companies listed at https://fortune.com/ranking/fortune500/

5. Isaac Getz and Laurent Marbacher, "The Altruistic Enterprise: How a Company Can Actually Succeed by Doing Good," *ESCP Impact Paper*, 2021, https://academ.escpeurope.eu/pub/IP%202021-02-EN.pdf

6. "DJSI Index Family," S&P Global, https://www.spglobal.com/esg/performance/indices/djsi-index-family

7. Ibid.

8. "Roche Named Among Top Three Most Sustainable Healthcare Companies In the Dow Jones Sustainability Indices," *GlobeNewswire*, December 15, 2023, https://www.globenewswire.com/news-release/2023/12/15/2796818/0/en/Roche-named-among-top-three-most-sustainable-healthcare-companies-in-the-Dow-Jones-Sustainability-Indices.html (NB: Roche maintained its top three ranking in 2023.)

9. "Roche," Yahoo Finance, accessed November 20, 2023, https://finance.yahoo.com/quote/rog.sw/

10. "IFRS S2 Climate-Related Disclosures," IFRS Foundation, https://www.ifrs.org/issued-standards/ifrs-sustainability-standards-navigator/ifrs-s2-climate-related-disclosures/

11. "FSB Plenary Meets in Frankfurt," Financial Stability Board, July 6, 2023, https://www.fsb.org/2023/07/fsb-plenary-meets-in-frankfurt/

12. Emmanuel Faber, *Ouvrire une Voie* (Editions Paulsen, 2022).

13. Annabelle Leproux, "L'ancien patron de Danone à Chamonix pour présenter son livre 'Ouvrir une voie,'" *Dauphine Libere*, February 24, 2022, https://www.ledauphine.com/culture-loisirs/2022/02/24/l-ancien-patron-de-danone-en-conference-au-majestic-pour-presenter-son-livre

14. "Raison d'Etre," Danone, https://www.danone.com/about-danone/sustainable-value-creation/danone-societe-a-mission.html

15. "Benefit Corporation," State of Utah, https://corporations.utah.gov/business-entities/benefit-corporation/

16. "Danone Raises 2017 EPS Forecast After WhiteWave Acquisition," Reuters, April 20, 2017, https://www.reuters.com/article/idUSKBN17M20P/

17. "DanoneWave Established as the Largest Public Benefit Corporation in the U.S.," P.R. Newswire, April 17, 2017, https://www.prnewswire.com/news-releases/danonewave-established-as-the-largest-public-benefit-corporation-in-the-us-300445182.html

18. Laurence Fletcher and Leila Abboud, "The Little-Known Activist Fund That Helped Topple Danone's CEO," *Financial Times*, March 24, 2021, https://www.ft.com/content/dd369552-8491-40a2-b83b-9a1b2e32407a

19. Peter Vanham, "Pro-ESG and Anti-ESG Activist Investors Have More in Common Than You Might Imagine," *Fortune*, December 8, 2022, https://fortune.com/2022/12/08/pro-anti-esg-activist-investors-common-ground-blackrock-bluebell-strive/

20. Dominique Vidalon, "Danone Clears Way for New CEO with Board Overhaul," Reuters, July 29, 2021, https://www.reuters.com/world/china/danone-clears-way-new-ceo-with-board-overhaul-2021-07-29/

21. "In 1789, a Nobleman Fleeing the French Revolution First Discovered the Healing Features of the Mineral Water Source in the Lake Geneva Town of Evian-les-Bains," Evian, Danone,

accessed March 27, 2024, https://www.danone.com/brands/waters/evian.html

22. "La Source Cachat," Ville d'Evian, https://ville-evian.fr/fr/culture/patrimoine/source-cachat

23. Dominique Vidalon and Pascale Denis, "Danone Eyeing Solid Evian Sales Thanks to Modernized Plant," Reuters, September 12, 2017, https://www.reuters.com/article/us-danone-evian-ceo-idUSKCN1BN11D/

24. "The Paris Agreement," United Nations Climate Change, consulted November 24, 2023, https://unfccc.int/process-and-meetings/the-paris-agreement

25. "For a Livable Climate: Net-Zero Commitments Must Be Backed by Credible Action," United Nations Climate Change, consulted November 24, 2023, https://www.un.org/en/climatechange/net-zero-coalition

26. "2030 Targets," Kunming-Montreal Global Diversity Framework, Convention on Biological Diversity, https://www.cbd.int/gbf/targets/

27. Interview with Claire Lund by Peter Vanham, September 25, 2023.

28. MAVA Foundation for Nature, accessed 6 March 2024, https://mava-foundation.org/history/

29. "Sustainable Economy Partners," MAVA Foundation, accessed March 20, 2024, https://mava-foundation.org/partners/#

30. "Our history As the Finance for Biodiversity Initiative (F4B)," *Nature Finance*, https://www.naturefinance.net/who-we-are/#history

31. Andre Hoffmann, "Mit dem Klimaschutzgesetz haben wir einen Berg zu erklimmen—und das ist gut so," *Handelszeitung*, June 15, 2023, https://www.handelszeitung.ch/politik/roche-vizeprasident-andre-hoffmann-mit-dem-klimaschutzgesetz-haben-wir-einen-berg-zu-erklimmen-und-das-ist-gut-so-610556

Chapter 7

1. "Concrete Needs to Lose Its Colossal Carbon Footprint," *Nature*, September 28, 2021, https://www.nature.com/articles/d41586-021-02612-5#ref-CR3

2. Vlaams-Brabant, "Domein Sinte Gitter," Landen, https://www.toerismevlaamsbrabant.be/producten/bezoeken/bezienswaardigheden/domein-sinte-gitter/

3. The UK Concrete Crisis, *Euronews*, September 11, 2023, https://www.euronews.com/2023/09/11/uk-concrete-crisis-what-is-raac-and-what-can-be-done-to-prevent-catastophe

4. Dmytro Katerusha, "Barriers to the Use of Recycled Concrete from the Perspective of Executing Companies and Possible Solution Approaches—Case Study Germany and Switzerland," *Resources Policy* 73, October 2021, https://www.sciencedirect.com/science/article/abs/pii/S0301420721002245

5. Andy Spoerri, Daniel J. Langa, Claudia R. Binder, and Roland W. Scholz, "Expert-Based Scenarios for Strategic Waste and Resource Management Planning—C&D Waste Recycling in the Canton of Zurich, Switzerland," *Resources, Conservation and Recycling* 53, no 10 (2009): 592–600, https://www.researchgate.net/publication/222428936_Expert-based_scenarios_for_strategic_waste_and_resource_management_planning-CD_waste_recycling_in_the_Canton_of_Zurich_Switzerland

6. "Bringing Embodied Carbon Upfront," World Green Business Council, accessed March 1, 2024, https://worldgbc.org/advancing-net-zero/embodied-carbon/

7. Richard Heede, "Carbon History of Holcim Ltd.," Climate Accountability Institute, July 7, 2022, https://callforclimatejustice.org/wp-content/uploads/Heede-Report.pdf

8. "Decarbonizing Building," Holcim, accessed March 1, 2024, https://www.holcim.com/what-we-do/decarbonizing-building

9. "Science Based Targets," https://sciencebasedtargets.org/

10. Esin Serin, "What Is Carbon Capture, Usage and Storage (CCUS) and What Role Can It Play in Tackling Climate Change?" London School of Economics, Grantham Research Institute on Climate Change and the Environment, March 12, 2023, https://www.lse.ac.uk/granthaminstitute/explainers/what-is-carbon-capture-and-storage-and-what-role-can-it-play-in-tackling-climate-change/

11. "Building One of Vienna's Most Energy-Efficient Schools with Low-Carbon Materials," Holcim, September 14, 2023, https://www.holcim.com/who-we-are/our-stories/vienna-energy-efficient-school

12. "Global Roll-Out of Green Concrete Ecopact Accelerating Sustainable and Circular Construction," Holcim, July 23, 2020, https://www.holcim.com/media/media-releases/global-launch-ecopact-green-concrete

13. "A World First: Holcim Produced 100% Recycled Clinker," Holcim, August 4, 2022, https://www.holcim.com/who-we-are/our-stories/recycled-clinker

14. "Delivering Record Results, Annual Report 2023," Holcim, published February 2024, https://www.holcim.com/investors/publications/annual-report-2023

15. "Holcim Supports Amazon's Shift to Sustainability with Ecopact," Holcim, February 2, 2023, https://www.holcim.com/who-we-are/our-stories/amazon-ecopact-data-centers

16. "Climate Change: No 'Credible Pathway' to 1.5C Limit, UNEP Warns," *UN News*, United Nations, October 27, 2022, https://news.un.org/en/story/2022/10/1129912

Chapter 8

1. "Company Purpose," Schneider Electric, accessed January 10, 2024, https://www.se.com/ww/en/about-us/company-purpose/

2. "Schneider S. A.," Encyclopedia.com, May 14, 2018, https://www.encyclopedia.com/social-sciences-and-law/economics-business-and-labor/businesses-and-occupations/schneider-sa

3. "Beaupréau. Jean-Pascal Tricoire, PDG de Schneider: 'Je me sens personnellement très Maugeois,'" *Le Courrier de l'Ouest*, October 15, 2019, https://www.ouest-france.fr/pays-de-la-loire/cholet-49300/beaupreau-jean-pascal-tricoire-pdg-de-schneider-je-me-sens-personnellement-tres-maugeois-915dd6b2-ef19-11e9-8deb-0cc47a644868

4. Mike Scott, "Top Company Profile: Schneider Electric Leads Decarbonizing Megatrend," Corporate Knights, January 25, 2021, https://www.corporateknights.com/leadership/top-company-profile-schneider-electric-leads-decarbonizing-megatrend25289/

5. "Key Figures, 2023," Schneider Electric, accessed March 25, 2024, https://www.se.com/ww/en/about-us/investor-relations/investment/key-figures.jsp

6. "Schneider Electric," Yahoo Finance, accessed March 25, 2024, https://finance.yahoo.com/quote/SU.PA/

7. "Sustainable Development Report 2003," Schneider Electric, https://ungc-production.s3.us-west-2.amazonaws.com/attachments/7491/original/Schneider_Sustainable_Development_Report.pdf?1282019191

8. Fortune 500, "2004, A Database of 50 years of Fortune's List of America's Largest Corporations," https://money.cnn.com/magazines/fortune/fortune500_archive/full/2004/

9. "Energy–Facts and Figures," Swiss Federal Council, accessed January 9, 2024, https://www.eda.admin.ch/aboutswitzerland/en/home/wirtschaft/energie/energie---fakten-und-zahlen.html

10. Ibid.

11. "Deux communes vaudoises choisissent Innergia pour atteindre l'indépendance énergétique et la neutralité carbone," Innergia, June 8, 2022, https://www.innergia.swiss/wp-content/uploads/2023/06/Innergia_RossTreyto_Communique depresse.pdf

12. Innergia Group Secures Funding from Swiss Environmentalist André Hoffmann, Innergia, 26 August 2022, https://www .innergia.swiss/wp-content/uploads/2022/08/Innergia_AH_ PR_260822_E.pdf

13. Jillian Ambrose, "Big Five Oil Companies to Reward Shareholders with Record Payouts," *The Guardian*, January 1, 2024, https://www.theguardian.com/business/2024/jan/01/ oil-companies-shareholders-payouts-bp-shell-chevron-exxonmobil-totalenergies

Chapter 9

1. "What Cog Will You Be?" HEC Graduation, June 2022, https://www.youtube.com/watch?v=BYIzclxtOLU

2. "Wake Up Call on the Environment: A Student Manifesto, Movement for an Ecological Awakening," accessed January 12, 2024, https://manifeste.pour-un-reveil-ecologique.org/en

3. "A Polytechnique et à Sciences Po, vent de contestation lors des remises de diplômes face à l'urgence climatique et sociale," *Le Monde*, June 24, 2022, https://www.lemonde.fr/campus/ article/2022/06/25/a-polytechnique-et-a-sciences-po-vent-de-contestation-lors-des-remises-de-diplomes-face-a-l-urgence-climatique-et-sociale_6132043_4401467.html

4. "AgroParisTech, ce n'était pas 'Martine à la ferme'…," *Le Point*, June 15, 2022, https://www.lepoint.fr/debats/agroparistech-ce-n-etait-pas-martine-a-la-ferme-15-06-2022-2479760_ 2.php#11

5. Anne-Fleur Goll and Pierre Salvadori, "France Inter," Radio France, July 19, 2022, https://www.radiofrance.fr/franceinter/ podcasts/un-monde-nouveau/un-monde-nouveau-du-lundi-18-juillet-2022-5329168

6. Ian Wylie, "What Generation Z Wants from a Business Masters," *Financial Times*, September 5, 2022, https://www.ft.com/ content/3f0ec54d-15b1-4974-8d5d-574f08788ef4

7. Ibid.

8. "INSEAD Ranked Second in the World in the FT's MBA Ranking in 2024." See "MBA 2024, Business School Rankings," *Financial Times*, February, 11, 2024, https://rankings.ft.com/rankings/2951/mba-2024

9. "The B Team Mission," B Team, accessed January 26, 2024, https://bteam.org/who-we-are/mission

10. "Cristiana Figueres," Global Optimism, accessed January 26, 2024, https://www.globaloptimism.com/christiana-figueres

11. "The Transformation Is Unstoppable," B Team, December 8, 2023, https://bteam.org/our-thinking/news/statement-the-transformation-is-unstoppable

12. Rachel Jetel, "What Is Systems Change?" World Resources Institute, November 4, 2022, https://www.wri.org/insights/systems-change-how-to-top-6-questions-answered

13. "The B Team History," The B Team, accessed January 26, 2024, https://bteam.org/who-we-are/our-history

14. "Manager mit Vorliebe für Afrika," *Spiegel*, April 10, 2007, https://www.spiegel.de/wirtschaft/puma-chef-zeitz-manager-mit-vorliebe-fuer-afrika-a-476391.html

15. "Puma Completes First Environmental Profit and Loss Account Which Values Impacts at €145 Million," Puma, November 16, 2011, https://about.puma.com/en/newsroom/news/puma-completes-first-environmental-profit-and-loss-account-which-values-impacts-eu

16. Ibid.

17. Jochen Zeitz, "Puma Completes First Environmental Profit and Loss Account," *The Guardian*, November 16, 2011, https://www.theguardian.com/sustainable-business/puma-completes-environmental-profit-and-loss

18. Jerry Garrett, "Harley-Davidsons to Remain Wisconsin-Made," *New York Times*, September 14, 2010, https://archive.nytimes.com/wheels.blogs.nytimes.com/2010/09/14/harley-davidsons-to-remain-wisconsin-made/

19. Roland Berger, "Harley-Davidson and the Rebranding of Rebellion," accessed January 29, 2024, https://www .rolandberger.com/en/Insights/Publications/Harley-Davidson-and-the-rebranding-of-rebellion.html

20. Jill Rothernberg, "Trump Loves Harley-Davidson. Do Harley Riders Love Him Back? *The Guardian*, March 13, 2017, https:// www.theguardian.com/us-news/2017/mar/13/donald-trump-harley-davidson-bikers-motorcycle

21. Timothy Puko, "Oil, Gas and Coal Interests Swarm Global Climate Summit in Dubai," *Washington Post*, December 5, 2024, https://www.washingtonpost.com/climate-environment/2023/12/05/un-climate-conference-dubai-oil-lobbyists/

22. "COP28 Letter," B Team, December 8, 2024, https://bteam .org/assets/reports/COP28-Letter.pdf

23. "Fiona Macklin," LinkedIn, December 2024, https://www .linkedin.com/feed/update/urn:li:activity:7135893604782252032/

24. Attracta Mooney, Aime Williams and Simeon Kerr, "Countries Reach 'Historic' COP28 Deal to Transition from Fossil Fuels," *Financial Times*, December 13, 2024, https://www.ft.com/content/3ffd821c-6200-4808-b16d-ac9cb2207f11

25. "COP28 Ends with Call to 'Transition Away' from Fossil Fuels; UN's Guterres Says Phaseout Is Inevitable." *UN News*, December 13, 2023, https://news.un.org/en/story/2023/12/1144742

26. "IKEA U.S. Announces Plans to Open Four New-Format Stores in 2024 and Shares Progress Made in FY23," IKEA US, January 19, 2024, https://www.ikea.com/us/en/newsroom/corporate-news/ikea-u-s-announces-plans-to-open-four-new-format-stores-in-2024-and-shares-progress-made-in-fy23-pubdaa657c0

27. "IKEA Sustainability Report FY23," IKEA, accessed January 28, 2024, https://www.ikea.com/global/en/images/IKEA_SUSTAINABILITY_Report_FY_23_20240125_94334a4bf3.pdf

28. "Wood Industry in Indonesia—Statistics & Facts," Statista, December 21, 2023, https://www.statista.com/topics/9466/wood-industry-in-indonesia/

29. "Vision, Culture and Values," IKEA, accessed January 28, 2024, https://ikea.jobs.cz/en/vision-culture-and-values/

30. "IKEA Expansion over the Decades," IKEA Museum, accessed January 28, 2024, https://ikeamuseum.com/en/explore/the-story-of-ikea/the-great-expansion/

31. "IWAY—The IKEA Supplier Code of Conduct, "IKEA," accessed January 28, 2024, https://www.ikea.com/global/en/our-business/how-we-work/iway-our-supplier-code-of-conduct/

32. Ibid.

33. "RetourMatras Can Now Recycle All Mattresses in the Netherlands," Ingka Investments, July 6, 2021, https://www.ingka.com/newsroom/retourmatras-can-now-recycle-all-mattresses-disposed-of-in-the-netherlands/

34. "INSEAD Global MBA Ranking Data, Business School Ratings," *Financial Times*, accessed March 21, 2024, https://rankings.ft.com/schools/135/insead/rankings/2951/mba-2024/ranking-data

35. "Poets & Quants' MBA Program of the Year for 2023: INSEAD," *Poets & Quants*, December 18, 2023, https://poetsandquants.com/2023/12/18/poetsquants-mba-program-of-the-year-for-2023-insead

Epilogue

1. Stanley Fields and Mark Johnston, "The Law of Evolution: Darwin, Wallace, and the Survival of the Fittest," in *Genetic Twists of Fate* (MIT Press, 2010).

2. Sarah Lacey and Cara Ocobock, "Forget 'Man the Hunter'—Physiological and Archaeological Evidence Rewrites Assumptions About a Gendered Division of Labor in Prehistoric Times," *The Conversation*, November 17, 2023, https://the conversation.com/forget-man-the-hunter-physiological-and-archaeological-evidence-rewrites-assumptions-about-a-gendered-division-of-labor-in-prehistoric-times-214347

3. Minouche Shafik, *What We Owe Each Other: A New Social Contract for a Better Society* (Princeton University Press, 2021).

4. "Why Retail 'Therapy' Makes You Feel Happier: The Brain-Based Effects of Shopping and Knowing the Signs of a Problem," Cleveland Clinic, January 20, 2021, https://health.clevelandclinic.org/retail-therapy-shopping-compulsion

5. Joseph Dodds, "The Psychology of Climate Anxiety," *BJPsych Bulletin* 45, no. 4 (August 2021): 222–26, https://www.ncbi.nlm.nih.gov/pmc/articles/PMC8499625/

Index

Note: Page numbers in italic refer to figures.

227